Praise for *The Duplex*

"[*Duplex* is] threatening to redefine the demographics of the cutting edge. . . . An ethnographic excursion into the thoughts of an often overlooked population."

Creem

"The tales of the *Duplex* . . . are modern-day versions of Chaucer's reports from the road to Canterbury; they resonate with a wry humor and a startling insight."

New York Times

"A shelter for the truly quirky remark, *Duplex* brings its odd, humorous and poignant sentiments to readers while avoiding a discomfiting divide between the laughers and the laughed-at. . . . A loving jokebook, a fine repository for aphoristic gems."

Village Voice

"Conversations easily move into associative flights of fancy . . . the affectionate way they're put together avoids any hint of condescension."

Chicago Reader

Duplex Planet

David Greenberger

Faber and Faber  BOSTON • LONDON

To the memory of Raymond J. Murphy

Published in the United States in 1994 by Faber and Faber, Inc., 50 Cross Street, Winchester, MA 01890

Library of Congress Cataloging-in-Publication Data

Duplex planet: everybody's asking who I was / edited by David Greenberger.

p. cm.

ISBN 0-571-19814-7

1. Aged men—Massachusetts—Boston—Humor. 2. Aged men—Massachusetts—Boston—Attitudes. 3. American wit and humor—Massachusetts—Boston. I. Greenberger, David. II. Duplex planet.

HQ1064.U6M3955 1994

305.26'0207—dc20 93-15820

CIP

Cover design by Mary Maurer (photo by David Greenberger)

Printed in the United States of America

Contents

DG: John, what's it like to be a bachelor all your life?

JOHN FALLON: Very good.

DG: What do you think about the artificial heart?

JOHN: Very good.

DG: That's the same answer you gave for the other question.

JOHN: Yeah.

dp

You want to know something about me? Read the Newport paper, they printed all my activities in the Newport paper. Get that paper and you'll know me like a book. *Bill LaGasse*

dp

Dishes are the hardest things to get clean nowadays. *Bill Niemi*

Introduction

A year out of art school I had an increasing desire to do something with the elderly. I had no idea what I had to offer or what to connect this desire with. Then I stumbled upon the Duplex Nursing Home, which I'd heard was looking for an activities director. I got the job; because I had no previous experience in this field, they lowered my pay by fifty cents an hour.

Almost immediately, I began asking the forty-five residents of the all-male home questions and writing down their answers. This soon resulted in a dozen or so 8½- by 11-inch typed pages, photocopied and stapled in one corner. Calling it *The Duplex Planet* with a modest, poorly-spaced banner across the top of the front page, I gathered all the residents together and passed out a copy to everyone. Within five minutes most of them had been discarded. The few copies that made it home with me, though, were read and enjoyed by friends. That's when it struck me: the audience for this was everybody *but* the people I was interviewing.

One of the things I wanted *The Duplex Planet* to be from the start was a picture of everyone who lived at the nursing home: people who were funny and people who were boring, people who were quiet, boastful, secretive, fascinating, sad, or slow, people who made sense and people who didn't. It's from the people who didn't always make sense that I've learned the most. They've given me a glimpse of one of the most feared aspects of the aging process. Being a friend to and observer of these people, the names of their conditions of deterioration mattered little to me; what did matter was that this was someone still very much alive, very interested in conversing, in entertaining or being entertained, in connecting with someone else.

The devil was working overtime in the Greyhound bus terminal. *Henry Turner*

dp

You don't get many prizes for nothin' in this life. *Bill Niemi*

dp

Many people in this world, they do small talking, very small talking. *Albert Dambrose*

dp

There's no use runnin' around actin' all mixed up—you've got to consult the calendar. *Arthur Wallace*

Everybody's askin' who I was.

Charlie Johanson

Jack Mudurian (left), Bill Sears

What would the title of your autobiography be?

The Stupid Life of Me.
Daphne Matthews

Love. *Andy Legrice*

I Ain't Got That Far Yet. (*DG: Is that the title?*) Yeah. *David Brewer*

A Champion of America!
Walter Kieran

Autobiography of Ernest Noyes Brookings. *Ernie Brookings*

My Total Workmanship.
Francis McElroy

A Veteran's Prerogative. *Abe Surgecoff*

Round the Corner with Bill.
Bill LaGasse

The Fallon Special. *John Fallon*

The Jack Mudurian Autobiography.
Jack Mudurian

This would probably be a title: The Life of Someone Named William.
Bill Niemi

What's the best thing that ever happened to you?

To be born lucky.

—Walter Kieran

Mindin' my own business and bein' a good boy. I've never been arrested and work everyday and don't owe anyone a nickel. And I never begged, borrowed or stealed anything. And I'm a retired civil service worker and a faithful church member.

—Francis McElroy

I got married.

—Larry Green

Love, fell in love.

—Andy Legrice

Got a divorce.

—John Fay

Bein' born, I s'pose.

—Frank Kanslasky

Comin' here.

—Gil Greene

November eleventh, 1918, in France, the First World War was over.

—Ernie Brookings

A child.

—David Brewer

Rice Krispies.

—*Jack Mudurian*

Money—when I became interested in money.

—*Bill LaGasse*

Stayin' single.

—*John Fallon*

Probably livin' the best you can after gettin' through school and everything, and bein' accepted by other people for something.

—*Bill Niemi*

Got my Social Security check. That's on a lifetime payroll, I am. I'm not working for no money, I'm just spending it. Well, some people might have a different opinion you know, a different idea.

—*Viljo Lehto*

I got a marksman medal in the National Guard. (*DG: That's the best thing?*) Yep. Peekskill.

—*Wally Baker*

The best thing that would happen would be if I get the hell outta here. You mean the best thing that happened in the past? (*DG: Yes.*) Jesus Christ! How the hell could I ever think of that?!

—*John Hodorowski*

Eddie Rutter: I don't know what to say.

Wally Baker: Well, say anything.

Eddie: Best thing that ever happened, I don't know what to name for that. I know there's a lot of things I wish I would've done, but I didn't do 'em.

DG: Like what?

I'd have quite a big one because I traveled so much. I'd call it Baltimore, because I was born in Baltimore. *Edna Hemion*

Heartthrobs. *Herman Seftel*

My Trials and Tribulations. *Janette Little*

The Past and the Present of My Life. *Dorothy Stein*

My Hardships of Life. *Elmer Wallach*

This Is My Life. *Dora Gurkewitz*

Yesterday and Today. *Ann Rapp*

A Truthful Story. *Sophie Terkel*

Married Life. *Ann Stark*

From Warren County On. *Lucille O'Brien*

The Life of Wallace L. Baker. *Wally Baker*

Myself and Glory. *Joe Ciarciaglino*

Onward, Onward Christian Soldiers. *Viljo Lehto*

dp

What do you think George Washington's voice sounded like?

JACK MUDURIAN: Coarse.

FRANK KANSLASKY: Like Jimmy Durante. Who can prove it? Can you prove it? No one can. Let it go. Jimmy Durante. Ever hear him talk? He didn't sound too bad. You don't want him to sound like Tarzan, do you?

LEO GERMINO: Sort of demanding. He was givin' orders. You can't know until you read his history. He might have had a voice just like us. He was a great man.

FRANCIS MCELROY: It was very outstanding and everybody liked to listen to his voice. He had a real cultured voice. And also, David, he done very little complaining, he was always jolly and cheerful to everyone.

BILL LAGASSE: George Washington had a booming voice.

ANDY LEGRICE: An orator. A dictator. A composer.

DAVID BREWER: It sounded like a dollar bill.

EDDIE: Oh, sometimes I wish I would've gone in the army sooner than I did, and so on, but that's about all.

Livin'. (*DG: What's the best part of livin'?*) Sleepin', eatin'.

—*Herbert Wilson*

Nothin' yet.

—*John Bitowski*

What don't you like?

Oh, I don't know. There's a lot goin' on in this life. I like makin' beds or somethin'. I don't like havin' a cold, I guess. Shovelin' snow or somethin' like that, I guess. We ain't got no beds made yet, anyway.

—*Herbie Caldwell*

Well now, let's see . . . sauerkraut and cabbage. That's all. I don't mind if they're on the plate—I don't have to eat 'em.

Well, I don't like people who boast too much, but I haven't met any in here.

I like most everything.

I never made good friends with a snake—I love dogs. I don't mind snakes if they stay on the ground. A big black snake lived in my backyard once. It was all right, I got used to him. I don't think I'd want to make friends with a rattlesnake. They used to have those at Blue Hill—that's not far from where I used to live in Ashmont—but I never met one face to face. There's too darn many people around now—the snakes'd be scared to death. But I'll take a good dog anytime. They're much smarter than people. We always kept a dog and a cat in the house at the same time.

—Robert Cleaves

I can't stand things if it's too exciting. It's not good to see things that are too exciting. It might upset you. I've got bad nerves, so it really works on me.

What I don't like? It all depends. I don't like mean people. I can't stand too exciting things on TV, either, you know. If it's too exciting I turn it off. Really works on my nerves.

—Gene Edwards

Nothing—I like everything. Is that a disappointment? I care for everyone, everyone I can. I haven't any enemies I know of. Of course we all have enemies, but we never mention them. We probably have enemies all over the world, but no one knows about them.

—William "Fergie" Ferguson

FRED MILLER: I think I like everything.

DG: How about snakes?

FRED: Oh, sure.

DG: Mosquitoes?

FRED: Oh, sure . . . I was in the Navy for four years, and a year in the Coast Guard. And I was captain of the East Boston ferry for five years.

I like everything. I don't care for fish and don't care for steaks. I will not eat it—fish is out of the question. I've been despising fish ever since I was a kid. Chicken? Forget it! That and fish—three things—chicken, liver and fish—forget it. I've got a long story about liver I can tell you—it's a bitch.

We were federalized March the tenth, 1941, and we went to Fort Dix. We opened that camp, it was closed since World War

BILL NIEMI: I think he had sort of like a —

FRANK KANSLASKY: Like a fag.

BILL: No! No! Kind of a soldiery and like a southern type of voice.

CHARLES SHEA: Bass-y.

PASQUALE TROIANO: You.

ABE SURGECOFF: Like a woman's voice. He talked softly and sweetly.

ERNIE BROOKINGS: The father of our country? (*Yes.*) Very loud and impressive.

I'm glad I got a pair of pants with a button on it. Christ, them zippers don't stay up, they slide right down. A button keeps it tight right around. *Walter Kieran*

dp

You know what I did this morn? I got out of bed in a hurry and I forgot to take my pajams off. I was in a hurry and forgot about it, put the pants on top of the pajams! *John Catrambone*

dp

What I like is those things you put your pants on, and it stretches right out and holds it in form. *Bernie Reagan*

dp

Dress me up in a slipper and pajamas, Jesus. *Herbie Caldwell*

dp

One and we opened it. And all they served us—all we could get was liver, liver, liver. Morning, noon and night. Breakfast, dinner and supper. I wish there was somebody here that was in that outfit—they would tell you this story, it's the truth. There was two outfits up there, the Yankee Division and the 372nd Regiment. The first time we got together since World War One and we opened up Fort Dix and stayed there until the bombin' of Pearl Harbor and then we went to New York to do guard duty. We had installations all over New York and parts of New Jersey, and I left the outfit in New York and went to Fort Wachooga, Arizona, and from there I went overseas with the 92nd Division. My campaign was all through Italy. And it was liver all that time, liver was all through all that. Meat was hard for people to get. Liver and fish was mostly all you could get. Your father could tell you about that. You could not get meat, unless you knew somebody, and then it was sky high. I never liked any of that stuff—liver, fish, all that stuff, all along. Nobody would put it in front of me—even my mother wouldn't.

—Ken Eglin

Oh, ah, let's see . . . Well, I ignore the things I don't like. It's easier that way. There's no sense in dwelling in dislikes, is there? It just makes it worse for yourself. Like if there's a taste you don't like, you don't think about it—you avoid it. Like there's certain foods I don't like. Certain combinations. Like macaroni and cheese—geez, I hate that. Broccoli on toast, cheese sandwiches—they're no good.

Places you don't like, you don't go to—you ignore them. You don't torture yourself by visiting places you don't like. Like you don't go visit a jail just because you don't like it.

You don't associate with people you don't like, do you? It's just aggravation. You go with people you're in harmony with. Everybody does that, for that matter.

—Mitch Krawcyznski

Some of these girls in here. I dislike all the pain in my belly. (*DG*: *What else?. Certain kinds of food, places, animals?)* I like all kinds of animals. Horses, cows . . . dogs . . . deer . . . squirrels . . . rabbits . . . cows, horses, goats . . . sheep and lamb.

I don't like snakes.

I don't like that TV noise.

—Arthur Labrack

I don't know. There's not much of anything I don't like. I was on a diet for a while and, uh, I used to get awful hungry. I was on a diet. I'd look at the other fellas eatin' a big meal, and I'd be havin' a little bit of meal. I didn't care about it too much, but I stuck to it.

—Bernie Reagan

There's a lot of things I do not like. Certain other things I do like.

—Frank Hooker

He's with me. There's only one police department I really like, and that's the M.D.C. They protected us when I was working as a lifeguard.

—Ken Eglin

I like everything. I worked in Naumkeg Mills—five years in Salem. And I worked ten years for the Salem Public Works Department. And I was errand boy for the Essex Institute in Salem. I was in *Javahead*, a movin' picture with Letrise Joy, Raymond Hamplin and Jacqueline Logan. Five weeks it took, in Salem, Massachusetts. They showed it all over the country, twenty years ago or more. I forget the date of it. It's a silent. It's hard to find now.

I like all my jobs. No fault to find at all.

—Walter Kieran

Dave, I just thought of two things—health and religion, those are two things I like—will you add those to my list? Thank ya, David. *Francis McElroy*

The Statue of Liberty is a female goddess, she's holdin' a light—that represents day. She's the Statue of Liberty, she tells where day is, she represents day. It was built by the French, all stone, stone statue. It's in New York, New York City, the harbor of New York City. It's been there a long time, many years. She's a giant woman representing day. *Harry Katz*

ANDY LEGRICE*:* Hats off, the American beauty!

DG*:* Who's the American beauty?

ANDY: Me!

I've been down on the farm and I don't like it. I'm a city girl from the word go. *Edna Hemion*

Viljo Lehto Says So, Part One

They used to say, "Oh, shit!" Back in the thirties when the railroad bridge broke down they'd say, "Oh, shit!" Now they say, "Bullshit." They changed it around. More modern, more pro-fesh-un-all.

If a crow would see my picture the crow would fly away.

You know what they used to call a moustache? A cookie duster. In the olden days, they had the cookies in a big jar and they'd get dusty.

They all look nice when they're young. Then they get old and wrinkled like me, with gray hair and everything goes down, hangs downward. You gotta have young blood, fresh blood. It's nice to be old people. When you're old like me you're senior citizens.

You got to be an honest man, you can't be a wing-dinger. Got to be an honest man, that's the way that I was brought up.

You got to speak clean American to me, otherwise I won't even speak to you.

I don't like police.

—*Tom Lavin*

There's all kinds of women around Harvard Square, and about ten or fifteen of 'em wearin' phony mustaches. They sold quite a few of them to the women. They used to pay eight dollars for those phony mustaches at the Harvard Cooperative Society run by the Harvard professors. All kinds of freaky women around Harvard Square. They're college girls. Harvard Square is a hangout.

I'm glad today is Monday. I hate Sunday. I didn't spend a nickel yesterday, did I? (*Bill Niemi: How would I know?*) I stayed in all day. I was tired and weary and worried. Wastin' my time in a nursing home. I came in when I was seventy-four. I should have never taken a lot of people's advice. Those goddamned cops, they'd say, "You've got money, go into a nursing home. Your people are dead, go into a nursing home." Of course, they meant well.

Not too many cops go into nursing homes. Some do, but not many. A lot of priests go into nursing homes, ones run by the church. One priest went in one and he committed suicide—he set the place on fire. Another priest retired and became a bartender. They called him Paddy the Priest. Everybody knew he was a priest, he had a religious look about him.

I never got pinched in my life and I hung out with all kinds of hoods. I hung out with Cambridge guys who would beat up drunken cops.

One guy from Cambridge had a bum eye. He was born that way. We used to call him Squint Eye. He had an upside-down pupil. But he got on the police force. He passed the exam because they didn't rule him cock-eyed, they ruled him squint-eyed. They transferred him to Harvard Square Station and he hung out with the Harvard students, and they educated him and he came in first on the police chief exam and he became the police chief of Cambridge. He was sixty-three years old then. Ted Lahey was his name.

He called me a horse thief in 1913. I didn't steal no goddamn horse! I was just looking at a Pierce Arrow, I was just askin' the chauffeur questions. And then he says, "Now Wallace, what are you askin' the chauffeur questions for? So you can steal the Pierce Arrow like you stole the horse and carriages?" and that started the fight. It was so fierce that we tore up Bob Moore's garden. I downed him with a flying' tackle, but he settled me with his cop's club and his belt.

He was a sonofabitch, a dirty bastard. He was a cruel cop. We used to fight with him a lot. But he worked himself up—he got educated and became police chief. I wasn't the only one who fought with him, the other guys would tangle with him too. It was because he'd start it. He'd insult you, he'd call you a horse thief or something. Him and two other cops were the three freshest cops in Cambridge.

I hung with all kinds of tough guys when I was young. Did you ever hang with a gang? They used to elect me captain of the baseball team. I always played shortstop. Some of the other guys on the team were tough guys too. We'd tangle with the fresh cops—Preshow, Ted Lahey and Frank Henry. Ted Lahey, he became police chief. That was because he got civilized and educated. My mother had Ted Lahey before the mayor three or four times for fightin' with me and the boys. He got suspended a couple times without pay. He was a big fat guy. Jesus Christ, when he got old he got so he could hardly walk. He had a lot of fat around the neck—three times the size of a normal guy's neck.

—Arthur Wallace

Thivierge is a French name. The only trouble with it is it's hard to write and hard to pronounce, but I've gotten so used to it I can write it right off. All my brothers changed their name. My

What's the smallest thing in the world and you can see it in the dark? (*DG: What is it?*) Lightning bug. They've got a dynamo in their rear end.

If you're too easy with the people, they'll climb all over you like mosquitos. You got to be tough on people, you got to enforce the law—I do. I see someone smokin' a cigarette or drinkin' beer, I say, "Hey! You're ruinin' your life!" And they believe me too. It's no wonder some of these people ain't got no stomach linin'!

Jealousy don't get you no place. Hatred don't get you no place, only downhill. You've gotta have full development.

My neighbor is an eighty-four-year-old woman and she's in no condition to drink beer—we don't even mention things like that! She's a widow and her husband was a police officer, very nice man.

My business is to talk a lot.

The Red Cross wants you to donate blood. Before they start on me, I tell them ahead of time, "You can take my blood but I'm full of wine and whiskey and mission stew and I don't want to hurt nobody."

The weatherman says it's gonna be cold tonight, so around midnight I'm gonna cook up a pork chop, in the moonlight. It doesn't cost much to cook in the moonlight.

I can be like a clown you know, but you can't always be clowning around, you've got to be regulated with others.

There's a lot of things you got to be responsible for, responsible for your own doings. Then if you do something wrong, they can put you up for a mental case.

brother Harry, my brother Stanley, my brother Eddie and my brother Charlie. They all changed it, all but me. They all had it changed to Norman. My sister Edith had her name changed to Norman too. I wanted to go over and change my name to Norman, but my father said no. He said, "That's my name and that's your name."

—Bill Thivierge

I remember when I was a boy growing up in Rome, New York, and we used to fly kites and there was this one kid who must've been the kite-flying champion of the world. He had a ball of string about a mile long. He'd get that kite way up there and it'd stay up all day long.

Of course, we didn't know anything about jet streams—when you're ten, twelve years old you don't think about those things.

—Bill Hughes

It's got to be religious music—that's the only way you'll get to heaven.

Viljo Lehto

Wally Baker

Do you sing in the shower?

They say a lot of people do, but I don't. *Leona Quant*

Never. Because when you go in the shower you go in there to wash up, and if you start singin' you're gonna miss somethin' and you're gonna come out and not be washed. *John Cipriano*

No, I worry about gettin' back out, even! I went head first one time, I had a black eye and everything. *Ida Harris*

No, no I don't sing. I just have radio, I listen to the radio. (*DG: You listen to the radio when you're in the shower?*) No. And I don't take a shower. *Rose Ellis*

No, I don't, ah, take showers, I just take baths. My daughter takes showers. But every once in a while if something hits me I'll start to sing an old song. That's why I was so thrilled to see the Bob Hope Show last night with all those actors I used to see. *Neil Henderson*

Why is music important?

(*Laughs*) Not to me, it ain't!

—Frank Kanslasky

Because it's very, very outstanding. It's important to make people feel better too.

—Leo Germino

I like it.

—Larry Green

Because it's the run of the country, and it's very popular among all people.

—Francis McElroy

Music is important because it's worth somethin'.

—Bill LaGasse

Well, it sort of relaxes a person's mind.

—Bill Niemi

Without it there'd be no happiness.

—Charles Shea

It's nice, it soothes you.

—George Stingel

All kinds of music I like and it calms me down. I've got a radio and a TV and when I get upset I turn on the radio.

—John Fay

Makes everybody happy.

—Austin Hartin

It brings melody to the people.

—Abe Surgecoff

Because it's essential to human enjoyment.

—Ernie Brookings

I don't care nothing about this cowboy music. It's got to be religious music—that's the only way you'll get to heaven. They don't like that cowboy music in the high church.

—Viljo Lehto

Well, to tell you the truth, it's kind of relaxing to hear it, and you can do a lot of dancing to it too.

—Wally Baker

Well, I think it's a great day-starter, starter of the day. Most people put their radio on and it brightens up the day. If we had a lot more music and less arguments, things would be a lot better—all over the world. In a lot of these countries, you aren't allowed to put music on.

—Howard Sherwood

Well, it's amusing to the people and I believe it's something that everybody likes.

—Eddie Rutter

It tunes up the system.

—Herman Seftel

We're lonely people and we live alone, so we like to have music.

—Dora Gurkewitz

It raises your spirits.

—Mary Pieszczoch

No. I don't want to get soap in my mouth. When I get in the shower I'm interested in getting myself clean. I do sing, but not in the shower.
Henry Turner.

TOM LAVIN: I'm trying to find my wife.

DG: Where is she?

TOM: Anywhere in the world . . . if I could just yell long enough . . . Blanche . . . that's B-L-A-N-C-H-E. She's a pain in the ass . . . and so am I.

DG: Tom, can you whistle?

TOM: Shit, no. *(Tries to whistle)*

DG: That's not bad.

TOM: By the time I get to whistle she'll be dead.

DG: Who?

TOM: Blanche, my wife.

DG: Could you whistle when you were a kid?

TOM: No, I could never whistle.

DG: You didn't do too bad when you just tried.

TOM: It's wicked. I can't make it sound good.

DG: Did you ever play any music?

TOM: No. Never even tried. I thought I was going to play the accordion, but I didn't think I was gonna get to do it . . . accordion.

DG: What stopped you?

TOM: Just the idea of . . .

DG: All that practicing?

TOM: Naw, I would have ate it up.

DG: How about singing?

TOM: Hell, no! . . . I think I would have liked to have been an accordion player.

Charlie Parker—he was all right! He was a quiet man, a very quiet man. But he wouldn't run from a fight. If you wanted to mess with him, he'd fight with you—he had to. Oh yeah, Charlie Parker. They called him Yardbird. He played the alto sax. Very good. He come up during the fifties. Before that, never heard of him. Les Young was gone—I don't mean dead, now—he wasn't playing around as much as usually—and in come Yardbird. Yardbird popped up with that crazy sax, oh Jesus Christ, he got so popular during the Korean War. He blew and blew and brought tears to your eyes. You couldn't help it—just like Pres, Father Young I call

I guess music is really a part of life.

—Dorothy Stein

It's cultural.

—Sophie Terkel

Calms the soul.

—George Vrooman

It soothes the nerves. And it keeps you from getting bored too. Of course, my radio was stolen from me.

—Henry Turner

Do you prefer fast songs or slow songs?

I prefer fast songs—live it up and be happy that way, Dave.

—Jack Mudurian

Slow songs are better. Fast songs are all right, but they're too rapid—you know what I mean? You ever see them sometimes on television?

—Leo Germino

Waltz. (*DG: Is that fast or slow?*) Slow, dreamy—dreamy waltz.

—Larry Green

I prefer a fast song. Am I right or wrong on that? (*DG: Either one is right, it's a matter of personal preference.*) And also, David, it could be a personal opinion.

—Francis McElroy

Fast. (*DG: Why?*) Because they're fast.

—*John Fallon*

DAVID BREWER: Slow songs.

DG: How come?

DAVID: How come? You know how come.

DG: No, I don't.

DAVID: You think about it.

Slow songs. Take your time, you'll live longer. Go too fast and you'll get worn out.

—*Andy Legrice*

Well I don't know, actually fast songs go too fast and slow songs go too slow. You have to find some happy medium, but I don't know if anyone's written that song yet.

—*Bill Niemi*

CHARLES SHEA: It's up to them.

DG: Who's them?

CHARLES: That are listening.

DG: Which do you prefer?

CHARLES: Medium.

Slow. I like beautiful music, I don't like fast hopscotch music.

—*Mary Pieszczoch*

Something in-between.

—*Ann Stark*

Slow songs, they're usually the old-fashioned ones.

—*Sadie Weinstein*

him—he'd blow and you'd go crazy. He was GOOD! He had his wild style that nobody else had. *Ken Eglin*

dp

DG: Abe, do you whistle?

ABE SURGECOFF: I don't know if I can. I never tried.

DG: You've *never* tried?

ABE: No, I've never tried.

DG: Who are your favorite whistlers in history?

ABE: President George Washington. Bob Hope—he used to whistle. Over in Korea he would . . . let's see now . . . Bing Crosby, his sons whistle. Let's see now . . . I can't think of any others right now. I'll tell you more later on.

dp

Bill Haley died? You're shittin' me! He was on that Queen for a Day—no! wait—that was Jack Dailey. I don't know who he is; I'm tryin' to think of him. They're all dyin'. *Ken Eglin*

dp

The Elvis Presley Argument, Part One

GEORGE VROOMAN: Elvis should've never opened his mouth!

DAPHNE MATTHEWS: The best thing he *did* was open his mouth!

DG: He's just trying to get your goat.

GEORGE: I know where her goat is pastured!

The worst thing that happened was Elvis Presley.

DAPHNE: No, the worst thing was my landlady died Tuesday.

GEORGE: Now you don't have to pay rent!

DAPHNE: Yes I do, I have to pay it to her daughter. She left her everything.

HENRY TURNER: You want this newspaper? You can have it. (*Leaves newspaper and walks away*)

DG: Thanks.

DAPHNE: Oh, there's Reagan's picture in the paper.

GEORGE: He stinks, just like Presley.

DAPHNE: Reagan stinks, I know that.

GEORGE: Elvis Presley wasn't born, he was hatched!

DAPHNE: You're gonna be wearin' that coffee if you keep it up! (*Laughs*)

Irving Berlin type of music, I always love his music. It brings back memories. (*DG: Did you ever see him?*) During the war he used to sing from the steps of city hall. He didn't have a good voice, it was a rasping voice, but it was what was behind the singing, the melody—that's what counted. That was back in 1919.

—*Herman Seftel*

DG: Which do you prefer, fast songs or slow songs?

ANDY LEGRICE: Both.

DG: When do you like the fast songs?

ANDY: When you're in heat.

DG: And when do you like the slow songs?

ANDY: When you're drinkin'! (*Laughs*)

Give me the slow ones, I don't like the fast ones. And I like to dance to the slow . . . songs . . . than to the fast ones.

—*Mary Monaco*

I was a very good dancer when I was young, back in the days when they used to pivot. As long as I had a good partner and the band played a fast tune, I would pivot the minute the band started playin' 'til the band quit—never stop, go all the way around the floor, you know? But I had to have a great partner, you know? But over the years I developed a little angina, so I get winded. So now I stick to the slow tunes. I'm a good jitterbug dancer and all that stuff, but now it's slow tunes. As long as it's moderate tempo. Anything fast—if I do—I tell my partner, whoever she might be, when I get tired we're gonna hit the deck, we're gonna sit down, 'cause I get winded, you know? Now my partner songs are tunes that are slow ones, but not that draggy stuff where you almost fall over you're walkin' so slow.

—*Tony Villano*

I don't dance, only the Polish hop, I love the Polish hop and I like it fast.

—Ethel Sweet

I kind of like fast music too, to listen to. To dance to—I get a little winded too!—so sometimes I prefer the slow-moving music.

—Mildred Makofsky

I like the fast music, especially the jitterbug tempo.

—Sylvia Novotny

I like slow songs like light opera because it's more easy to understand and it's more relaxing than a fast tempo, as far as I'm concerned.

—Henry Turner

Makes no difference. There's a lot of fast songs and there's a lot of slow songs too. It all depends on how fast you put them on the record player.

—Wally Baker

Well, I like them slow. That fast jazz is not for me.

—Howard Sherwood

I would say just ordinary music, just regular music, the way it's played.

—Ed Rogers

It depends upon the nature of the music. Slow lasts longer than fast.

—Ernie Brookings

GEORGE: Now my stomach's upset, talkin' about Elvis Presley.

DAPHNE: Oh! Will you—go take a bath on Erie Boulevard! (*To DG:*) Did you see how fat he got in the seventies? He used to be so slim and trim and then he got to be as big as a house. They said that after Priscilla left he really went downhill. And his mother dyin' didn't help any.

Brrrrr—it's cold!

GEORGE: Talkin' about Elvis Presley ought to keep you warm!

DAPHNE: If he was here I'd be warm because I'd rush over and hug him!

Eat your toast!

GEORGE: I can't eat my toast, I lost my appetite talking about Elvis Presley.

DAPHNE: Oh! I'm gonna turn you upside down and shake you! (*To DG:*) You can have all the change that falls out, I'll take the dollars. (*Laughs*)

dp

DOROTHEA BROWNELL: I know nothing whatsoever about Elvis Presley. I never heard him sing—I never even *heard* of him until all this present day business of people seein' him and so forth. I didn't know anything from him.

DG: Even from the newspapers back in the fifties? You knew he was around—you knew the name—

DOROTHEA: I don't know whether I did or not. It made no impression, no impression whatsoever.

DG: The movies, none of it—

DOROTHEA: Oh, I didn't go to the movies, I haven't been to a movie in years. And I had no television, so of course I never saw any of that. But I heard people saying' that he was loathsome, that his actions and such were beneath contempt, but I don't know anything about it, nothing personally. I never heard him sing.

DG: Never?

DOROTHEA: Never.

DG: Even on the radio?

DOROTHEA: Nooooo!

DG: Hmmm.

DOROTHEA: Nope.

dp

What can you tell me about the Beatles?

All I know is they came from England! (*Laughs*) (*DG: Why's that funny?*) Oh, it ain't funny. To tell you the truth, I didn't care too much about 'em. I guess one of 'em, or a couple of 'em, was drug addicts too. Remember that? I didn't know too much about 'em, but people told me they were drug addicts, a couple of 'em.

—Fred Delap

DAPHNE MATTHEWS: My favorite Beatle song was "Let It Be." The first time I heard that it was so lovely, oh, I loved it!

I liked 'em, they're a great group. I liked their hair styles. My mother and father didn't care for 'em—my mother and father couldn't stand 'em! My mother said she was ashamed of what her country put out.

DG: She's English?

DAPHNE: Yes, definitely. I saw their movies that they made.

DG: What'd you think of them?

DAPHNE: I liked 'em, they're very good. They had one called "Help" and "A Hard Day's Night," "Sergeant Pepper's Lonely Heart's Club Band," "Helter Skelter." I used to ride on that in England, the Helter Skelter, it was something similar to a slide, like a sliding board the kids slide on today.

They're singers, they come from England and the women were screamin' over 'em. I couldn't see nothin' in it—they didn't do anything for me.

—George Vrooman

Do they talk? (*DG: Sure they talk—they sing, too.*) They sing, huh? Then put that down—"The Beatles sing."

—*Leo Germino*

They're a whaddayacallit, a music, a whaddyacallit—they're in the music business. That's what you call rock and roll. They're on the, ah, music—show business—they were on the radio.

—*Ed Rogers*

LARRY GREEN: The Beatles were good singers. They're a good quartet. "Apple Blossom Time," "God Bless America"—Kate Smith sang that, she sang it way down yonder in New Orleans. I'll be seeing you in apple blossom time. You are my sunshine, my only sunshine. God bless America, land of the free, stand beside us and guide us—I forget all the words—I used to know them. "Apple Blossom Time," "God Bless America."

DG: What did the Beatles look like?

LARRY: Oh geez, they was elderly. I don't know, it's been a long time since I've seen 'em. They make good records. I'll be seeing you in apple blossom time. Ain't misbehavin', savin' my love for you. Molly and me, baby makes three.

DG: What were the Beatles' names?

LARRY: Moe and Joe—the Beatles! One got shot, didn't he?

DG: Yes.

LARRY: Killed him outright?

DG: Yes.

LARRY: Oh Jesus, that's tough. Was it a fight over a card game? Poker?

DG: No, it was just someone crazy.

LARRY: Ohhh, that's too bad. They were good. . . . Did you ever hear the Mills Brothers?

DG: Boy, a whole big chunk of popular culture.

DOROTHEA: That's right, cut right out!

dp

FRANK HOOKER: Elvis Presley was born in Nashville, Tennessee. Great singer. He was in the United States Army.

HAROLD FARRINGTON: He was a truck driver, wasn't he?

FRANK: Yep.

BILL SEARS: He was a boxer too, wasn't he?

HAROLD: Was he?

KEN EGLIN: He was nothin' when he started, but he built himself up.

FRANK: When he was in the United States Army.

BILL NIEMI: He had a big mansion there, didn't he, in Chattanooga, Nashville, Tennessee. Then he got sick, some kind of rheumatic fever. Then he was takin' dope, some kind of a dope addict.

KEN: That's what I don't believe.

BILL: Well, he was takin' dope. It must be true because they had it on the news at the time of his passin' away.

KEN: Him, Brenda Lee and Tom Jones were all the ones I was keepin' records on. Tom Jones is still goin'. Brenda Lee's retired I guess . . . or married . . . fool . . . And Nat "King" Cole, don't leave him out, he was fabulous. I didn't like the way they put his picture in the paper in his casket. He looked horrible. I didn't like that at all.

BILL: That's illegal, isn't it, to show pictures of people in their caskets before they're buried? It's alright for relatives to take pictures at the graveside.

The Elvis Presley Argument, Part Two

GEORGE VROOMAN: Elvis had no pelvis!

DAPHNE MATTHEWS: (*Laughs*) Here we go again!

DG: Oh good, part two of the Elvis argument! I'm ready for it!

Is it a fraternal organization?

—Ernie Brookings

To be honest with you, I'm a very frugal living person. All I have to say about the Beatles is they sing too loud. To be honest with you, I think they should be arrested for disturbin' the peace. And here's something about the politics: I quit the Republican party because Reagan made a Democrat out of me. We all have the same heavenly father, but he's not doin' anything about the homeless people. How would he like to be a homeless person sleeping on the sidewalk and not bein' able to take a bath? And I'm definitely not voting for Pat Robertson—he wants to end Social Security. What are the homeless people and the mentally ill going to do? What are they supposed to do to live—starve to death?

—Henry Turner

They were a musical organization. They're still playin', aren't they? They were in Hollywood for a while, making pictures. It was on television that one of them was murdered in New York, that John Lennon. They'll probably have to reorganize the whole dance band.

—Bill Niemi

Sweet beetles, oh they're the sweetest little animal you ever saw. They come right up to you and chew up the ice cream for you. And they hand the pecans to you. And those pecans aren't celluloid either, they're the real thing.

—Fergie

Don't know about 'em, actually. That's not a good question to ask me. Except that they were young men from Liverpool, England, and unemployed at the time. They were poor young boys—fifteen, sixteen—kicking the bricks in Liverpool, England, and they either found, stole or were given some cheap instruments.

I think I explained to you once why that should be pronounced Lie-verpool. (*DG: Why is it pronounced Lie-verpool?*) Oh, I didn't explain it to you. Well, it's named after a lake which is a fairly large lake to the northeast of the city, and it's inhabited by birds which are called livers—not livers, which is an organ of the body. They're liverbirds—you underline the "i" to emphasize it, pronounced like lie. It's kind of a fish-eating water bird, something like a cormorant.

—*Bill Hughes*

Yeah, yeah, yeah, yeah, yeah, yeah! I was one of their fans. Ringo! They're all dead, I think. What, was there five of them? They're all gone.

—*Frank Wisnewski*

They were pretty good—the greatest team goin'—a quartet. I guess they made their money and went home. They had long hair and looked pretty good—the girls liked 'em. They had a guitar and another electric guitar, and of course you couldn't tell the names of the songs—I was sleepin' most of the time when he said 'em.

One of the Beatles got shot. And he died. He was syndicated—turned to ashes. That was the end of him. A gunman shot him. Thirty-fourth street. Gunman shot him because he spit on his shoe and he said it wasn't him, it was his brother and he made a mistake. That's all I know. The rest of them are still around, playin' on the stage. They went to the funeral, I guess, when he died. He was syndicated.

—*Bill LaGasse*

DAPHNE: I think it's too much of a coincidence, because his mother died when she was forty-two on August fourteenth, and he died when *he* was forty-two, on August fifteenth—it's too much of a coincidence, and that's why I won't believe he's dead.

He was born in 1935, on January eighth.

JEANNE M.: Who?

DG: Elvis.

JEANNE: Yeah, she's right.

DAPHNE: No way in the world he can be dead! I won't believe it, too much of a coincidence.

GEORGE: (*Sings:*) Elvis had no pelvis!

DAPHNE: Ha! He used to shake it all the time!

GEORGE: (*Grumbles/laughs*)

DAPHNE: He's very good looking and he could really act.

GEORGE: He looked like a horse.

DAPHNE: Ah, baloney! He was very handsome, he didn't look like no horse.

JEANNE: Who said that?

DAPHNE: He did! (*Points at George*)

JEANNE: I don't like people who throw stones, especially when they live in glass houses! I'll spank you and hurt you!

DAPHNE: Pour a gallon of milk on his head!

JEANNE: That was a surly comment, George. Now apologize.

GEORGE: I can't help it if he looked like a horse!

JEANNE: He was a nice looking man, George.

DAPHNE: Oh yeah, very handsome.

DG: You're outnumbered on this one, George.

DAPHNE: Two to one. (*Gets up from table to go get coffee*)

GEORGE: There's more women than men, and they all like Elvis.

JEANNE: Now don't get her going. She knows in her head that he's really dead, but won't admit it in her heart. They cut that man up into a million pieces to find out how much drugs he took.

DG: Herbie, can you play the piano?

HERB CALDWELL: Couple'a notes, that's all.

I never seen them. They're the English ones, ain't they? I heard one song of them, but I don't know what one it was, someone said it was the Beatles. I never saw them on television. I just woke up a few minutes ago.

—*George Stingel*

I don't know nothin' about the Beatles—I can tell you more about the Salem Fire. June 25th, 1914. It burned seven days and seven nights. We had doughnuts and coffee by the Salvation Army. I also wrote a book on the Salem Fire. Worked with the Salem Public Works Department, fifteen years.

—*Walter Kieran*

(Singing) I wanna hold your hand! I wanna hold your hand! I like the Beatles, Rolling Stones. Roll out the barrel, we'll have a barrel of fun!

—*Pasquale Troiano*

I don't know who they are—that's before my time. You mean the real beetles, like the Japanese beetles? (*DG: No.*) Oh, you mean the singers from England. I don't know about them. Are they still in business? (*DG: No.*) They say when a person is born he is given the gift of life and he should live to the fullest because someday it'll be taken back. That's when you're dead.

—*Joe Ciarciaglino*

I don't know much about the Beatles. They chirp and play around. I'm supposed to have coffee, but I don't know where it is.

—*Herbie Caldwell*

They're good singers. They're good Americans.

—*Andy Legrice*

I can tell you what I like about 'em and what I don't. They seemed to stay original—I like that. There's so much I don't like about 'em though—like harmony, I don't like that harmony. I don't give a damn about their looks—that thing don't bother me—I'm just talking about their sound. I like the fact that they're original, but I don't like the songwriting.

—Walter McGeorge

Oh, I can't remember that far back! I used to go to musicals in New York. There's no place like New York—my father said that, and his daughter says it now.

—Edna Hemion

I can't tell you about the Beatles—I don't know a thing about them. I never worked for them and they never worked for me.

—John Lowthers

That's a different kind of music than regular music. It's different than the ordinary, regular music. It's a different type, that's all, it's a different type of music than the regular music they have on. *Ed Rogers (in response to hearing "Are You Experienced?" by Jimi Hendrix on the radio)*

I wish *I* knew a hundred songs—Frank Sinatra knows a hundred songs.
Jack Mudurian

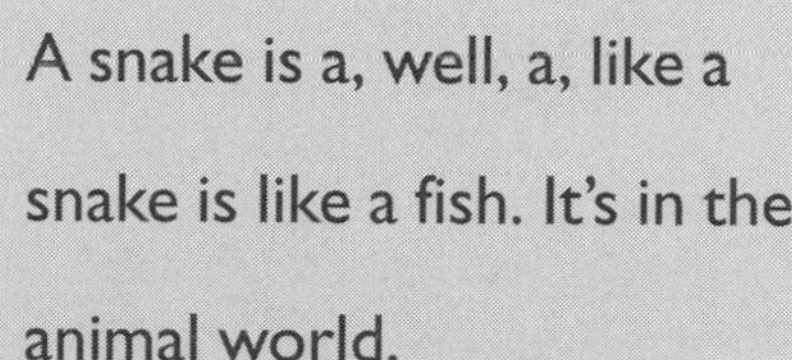

A snake is a, well, a, like a snake is like a fish. It's in the animal world.

Ed Rogers

Daphne Matthews

I don't know much about snakes. They grow big, big enough to devour a man; I've seen 'em that big. Cars run over 'em and don't harm 'em. I don't think they eat human. They eat rodents and stuff like that, anything they can get. I have a friend that gets the venom out of 'em. Pushes it under the tooth. He gets barrels of it from them. Venom from snakes. Then he sells it. I don't know who buys it.

—Bill LaGasse

There's such a thing as poisonous snakes and water snakes. I believe my friend here (*points to Ken Eglin*) calls them monsters. Nothing more I can tell you about snakes, not being very familiar with them.

—John Lowthers

I've seen 'em but I don't know anything about 'em. How'm I gonna tell you about something I don't know anything about? I saw one once in my life, up in a cemetery. If you asked me about something I knew about, that'd be different.

—Walter Kieran

There's different varieties of snakes. In some countries they call them reptiles, and not snakes, for some reason, and, ah, some snakes, ah, grass snakes, they live in the grass and they keep an eye on the grass, in case people malign it, you know, start desecratin' the grass or something—they get mad at the grass or something—they attack people like that. They bite them. Sometimes they curl around their feet. And if the person has their hand down, pulling up the grass, they're liable to curl around their wrist. And if they entwine themselves around the person's wrist, that interferes with your breathing, they're liable to choke to death.

Then there's water snakes and rattlesnakes and boa constrictors. Those water snakes, some of them are poisonous like they claim rattlesnakes are. And boa constrictors eat people

What kind of an animal would you like to be if you had to be one?

ERNIE BROOKINGS: A canine, if I had to be one. A dog gives protection to the home, they're always alert and will bark to announce trespassers are there. And if necessary, if the trespassers are distant from the home, the dog will travel home and bark to the master and bring him back to where the trespassers are.

LEO GERMINO: A black tiger, then I'd go after my enemies! No, I'm just kiddin' ya, I wouldn't want to be an animal, I'd rather be a human being. I pity the animals. (*DG: Why?*) Well, I'd rather be a sparrow or a pigeon—something with wings—that's the only way you get to heaven, with wings. I'm just kiddin' ya.

whole, they're very dangerous. They have some in this country down south and they're very prominent down in South America, in El Salvador and Nicaragua and Panama and Brazil. They're very big snakes.

Then when people go in the service they can be very dangerous, especially when they get sent to tropical areas. They've got to be careful when they go out in the jungle and the swamps. You don't know what kind of snakes and animals you're going to meet out there. The jungle is very dangerous. It grows wild and tries to engulf civilized sections into its grasp.

—*Bill Niemi*

Oh boy, do I love those things! I'm not afraid of those things. Now, the most deadly snake that you've got in the world is the one that killed Cleopatra and now that snake is out in Egypt. You've got all different types of snakes. You've got the boa constrictor, that's mostly in Brazil—no, not Brazil, Burma. They'll squeeze you to death. He stays on top of a tree and he will see you and come down, very quietly come down and wrap himself around you and there's no out—he'll squeeze you to death.

Then you've got the python. A python is bad in one way—he'll wrap himself around you and bite you—he can kill you. You see pythons in Africa.

Now, the most deadly snake is a bush whack—they call it that. It's in Africa. The natives will tell you, "Don't go down that path!" The bush whack will come down out of the tree. If he sees you comin' he'll lay on a branch and wait and let the group go by, and the last person goes by, they will drop right on 'em. And that's the end of 'em. He will squeeze you in every direction, until your head is a pin—that's all that's left. Your nails'll fall out, your tongue, everything. He just squeezes you until there's nothing left and then crawls off and waits for another sucker—that's if the natives don't get to him first. These natives, they know the grounds, where all these things are. They know where the flying snakes are—you've heard of flying

JOHN LOWTHERS: Why, ah, sort of a muskrat. They eat just nothin' but corn.

DG: You like corn a lot?

JOHN: Yes, just corn.

DG: That's all you'd eat?

JOHN: Yes, just corn.

DG: That's if you were a muskrat—do you like corn now, as a human?

JOHN: No, I don't think I care for corn.

WALTER MCGEORGE: A dog. They're domestic.

JOHN FALLON: A donkey. (*DG: Why?*) Just for the hell of it.

FRANCIS MCELROY: I'd like to be a bear! They're gentle, but when they get mad they're bad actors—if anyone disturbs 'em, they're up in arms.

WALTER KIERAN: A zebra. (*DG: Why?*) Because they're very odd.

JACK MUDURIAN: A horse, because I like Johnny MacBrown—I want him to be my rider and I'd take him anywhere in the world without being hurt. (*DG: Who's Johnny MacBrown?*) He's a cowboy on the movie screen, he's in the westerns.

I don't want to be a draft horse, I want to be a saddle horse, Dave.

BILL NIEMI: If I had to be an animal? (*DG: Yes.*). . . Probably it would be a good thing to be a cow. You'd probably get taken care of, you know. You'd probably be taken out to pasture to get your food, and you'd be brought back to the barn at certain times to be milked.

GIL GREENE: A cheetah. (*DG: Why a cheetah?*) It's supposed to be the fastest animal in the world.

That's a question psychiatrists ask, about what kind of animal you want to be.

BILL LAGASSE: An ape.

DG: Why?

BILL: I don't know.

DG: What do you like about apes?

BILL: Nothin'.

snakes—a flying snake, they just leave the tree, just jump and fly through the air. A section of the wind will carry them and whatever's in the way will stop them—for the time being. Now see, these natives know where the flying snakes are, they'll tell you where not to go. "Dangerous! Dangerous!", and they point and back away and you look up and you see what they mean.

I've been bit—well, slightly bit—by a rattlesnake. I was tryin' to climb up the Watchupa Peak in Fort Watchupa, Arizona. I was in the army in training. I threw my rifle up on top of the ledge, got my fingers and I was pullin' myself up and I heard that *ss-s-s-s-s*, that sizzle, and I froze and I pulled myself up so I could see, I got up chin high, so as I could see where that sizzle was comin' from. And I looked left and right and saw the rattler and it bit me—it didn't get a good bite—it just nipped me, in the arm. And I let go and went down about thirty feet to the bottom. I just laid there. I just couldn't move my left arm. I thought sure I was dead and I heard someone say, "Don't move, just lay still." And I looked up and there's Billy, Sergeant Dunkin. He fired his pistol and killed the rattler. That actually happened to me, 1942—no, put 1943. I have run into a lot of rattlesnakes in my days—but not that way. Over here at Blue Hill they've got rattlesnakes. People don't realize that.

—*Ken Eglin*

Snakes were dangerous when I was riding on a locomotive and we stopped to load up the engine with water and, ah, we had to shut our windows on the locomotive.

A snake is in the bush and then he jumps up about twenty feet high. Some people have been caught by going off the train, snake bites. As the train would go by there the snakes would jump up. They attacked two guys while the window was open. The engineer wanted at least two persons to come with him when he would go by the station because he was afraid he might be bitten because they roam around. The MPs were at the station. The MPs told the engineer that it might not be good to stop there and he should go to the next station and get loaded. Peopled hated to stop at that station.

I'm not too good with these stories.

—*Abe Surgecoff*

They're bad. They cut the wind out of you. They can snap your neck. They'll choke you. (*DG: Why would they do that?*) For the honor.

I had a fish one time, dove out of the water on top of the deck. I swung the axe on him.

—*Fred Miller*

A snake is the most ferocious, most unpredictable animal alive. No friends. A copperhead is so vicious they strike at sound. A black snake will kill their own mother for a berry. They love berries.

—*Walter McGeorge*

They can't close their eyes. They can't close their eyes because they ain't got any eyelids. And they can't hear, neither. They're not nice to look at. A boa constrictor squeezes animals and people to death if it's disagreeable with them, if they don't come to an eye-to-eye understanding with them. There's something else about snakes, I can't quite think of it. . . . They die easily, even when hurt a little bit. I think I found that out on TV. Only three percent of the snakes in the world are poisonous. That's what I found out.

—*Jack Mudurian*

I wonder about snakes, too. They kill people, that's what happens. That's why everybody runs from them. They come down south and they come up here, too. How come they don't last in the winter, though?

—*David Brewer*

DG: Then why do you want to be one?

BILL: I don't know.

DG: But you're sure you want to be one?

BILL: Yes.

DG: Okay.

HARRY KATZ: A cat because my name is Katz. A cat is a peaceful animal, it don't harm nobody.

HAROLD FARRINGTON: A female hyena.

How close can you get to a penguin?

GEORGE VROOMAN: Probably about five feet.

DAPHNE MATTHEWS: They're terrific, aren't they? I'd like to get as close as I can. I'd like to go up and hug 'em, they're so cute!

WALTER KIERAN: Grab 'em.

DG: You can get that close?

WALTER: Sure!

DG: Why would you want to grab one?

WALTER: For a souvenir.

DG: Can they be trained?

WALTER: Sure!

BILL NIEMI: Penguin?! Oh, my God! You'd have to go way down to the South Pole!

ERNIE BROOKINGS: It all depends upon the location. If in a nearby tree, you can get very close—if the penguins were on one of the branches you could get very close.

VILJO LEHTO: Sometimes you can get about two inches, but you can't breathe too close to 'em though, 'cause they don't like that when you're breathin'.

dp

Watch out for the rattle.

—Tom Lavin

That was years ago. I was in the army, twenty years. I'm on my own now, I'm no longer in the army. I'm retired, I'm an old soldier.

—John Colton

Oh, I'd be afraid of them, Dave. The only ones I ever saw were only about a foot long. I don't know what you call them, Dave. They stay in marshland. I went to the Middlesex Zoo with a girl, she took me out there, and there's a big boa out there, a big snake. They're in a glass cage. One of them could swallow a man, crush and swallow him. They don't have them in this country except in zoos, but I'd be afraid of 'em. I don't like snakes at all.

—George Stingel

They're one of the finest things in the world, but they're one of the finest things to leave alone. Don't bother them and they won't bother you.

I know a snake is very helpful in some instances and very destructful in others. And I suppose you're going to say, "Such as," or, "What is one and what is the other?" There's many different types of snakes. Grass snakes and ground snakes. G-R-O-U-N-D, ground snakes. And tree snakes, they go up trees. They'll go up some of the tallest trees we've got—poplar trees. We've got plenty of them. We've got them up north and we've got them down south. They're big around as our body, but they run forty, fifty feet up in the air. Sixty-eight to seventy feet is the tallest poplar tree. A poplar tree is as big around as our body, all the way up. Up to sixty-six, seventy feet, that's the tallest. There may be some a little taller, but not much, seventy-two, seventy-four feet.

A tree snake can circle a poplar tree. They'll go around it just like they can go around your body. You don't bother them, they won't bother you. You can talk to a snake and a snake will nod to you yes or no, if you ask them a single question that's a human question, it may not be an animal question, but it may be about animals. Of course, it's according to what kind of a snake you're talking to. If it's a grass snake or a tree snake it's altogether different. A tree snake can go up a tree just like an animal. Just like a bird flies, a hummingbird.

There are many different kinds of snakes. I couldn't give you any exact number, but there's hundreds of different kinds. Grass snakes and . . . R-I-D-G-E, ridge snakes, where you have ridgewood. You know what a ridgewood is? R-I-D-G-E. Ridgewood is, it's a southern wood, down around Bermuda, there's many of those tall trees. Poplar trees they call them. P-O-P-U-L-A-R. They start about as big as our body, I mean about as big as a woman's body. Most women are not as tall as a man. Most men are six-foot, six-foot-four and six-foot-six. They run different sizes, I run only five-foot-eight, but most men and women are much taller than I am. I'm one of the shortest, of the men department. And then women are the same, they run up five-foot-ten, -eleven, -twelve and six-foot. Many women aren't as tall as the men, but they are very near—within a foot . . .

There's many different kinds of snakes. There's grass snakes and tree snakes. If it's a tree snake it can wind around a poplar tree, just like it's your body. Ridge snakes, they're more like the size of your arm or your leg. It's a southern snake, a coral snake. Down around the Bahamas, the Bahermas, Bermuda. They don't do anything. They're about as big as from your wrist to your elbow to your shoulder. Their head is like the size of your fist. And it runs from there to your elbow and your shoulder and the length of your body, about five-foot-eleven or six-foot. Some of them will run about eighteen-foot.

I don't know too much about them. They look at you and not at you and if you speak to a snake, a snake'll speak to you.

What can you tell me about the behavior of fish?

The behavior of fish is like any other creature, they have their ups and their downs. Some are faster than others, but that doesn't always make them win you know, just because they're faster. They might be faster in one direction, but it might not be the right direction.

They are very, very careful that they do not make any mistakes. Of course, they make mistakes like anyone, but they try not to. But they make a mistake just the same. Different kinds of mistakes, too many to mention. *Fergie*

A fish has no, ah, no feet. That's all I know. *Ed Poindexter*

They're wild. *John Fallon*

They eat worms. *Larry Green*

They're orderly. *Harry Katz*

Normally, they swim in the water. Some jump out of the water. Sharks are mammoth, and whales. And trout are found in brooks. Another kind of fish is alewives. Fish lay eggs and the eggs hatch, is that true? (*DG: I believe so.*) Some of the fish are very active and can jump out of the water. They swim in schools. *Ernie Brookings*

Well, the mother's down there schoolin' for the small children. And, ah, she catches them and some of them they eat, of the smallest schools. *Abe Surgecoff*

The behavior of fish is when they're in the water, floatin' around. *Leo Germino*

Fish is a great creature. And it's also a great brain food. And it's always liked by everyone. And it's also a great dish to eat at any time. *Francis McElroy*

Any special fish you want me to talk about? (*DG: Any kind.*) All I know is that fish bite you, don't they? They've got teeth, they bite you. I wish I could tell you more, but I just can't think of what to say. *Gene Edwards*

I eat fish, I don't want to know about their behavior. *Frank Wisnewski*

There's no behavior on fish. *Waldo Friesz*

They're always spawnin', always makin' whoopee. That's why there's so many of 'em, that's all they do. It's good sport, fishin'. *Andy Legrice*

Well, they're lively when they're in the water, but when you take them out they're dead. *Walter Kieran*

C-O-B-R-A. A cobra is as big as your left hand or your right hand and from there it's as big as your arm, the muscles, and the muscles of your upper arm, and they may be four to six feet long.

There's different lengths of snakes, there's different types of snakes. How many, God only knows. Our Lord Jesus Christ knows. If you saw him, he could tell you. It's very rare that you see Our Lord Jesus Christ. Very, very rare . . . It's very rare that you see a snake.

—Fergie

Why, ah, they're sittin' in the wind-up, in the circle—ah, coiled up—and they'll strike out. They used to go for mice in the fields. They'd swallow a whole goat. Or sheep.

We used to have a musical instrument, a reed, and we'd play it and they'd sit up and move around—go from side to side. And, ah, the only way to catch them is with traps. Put bait in them, put a mouse in there and they'll strike at the mouse and the thing will come down and clamp on their head.

They had mice too, that danced to music. They danced around. We have a cat here that's a good mouser. He'd wait beside the hole and I covered up the hole with a piece of tin. When the mice is away the cat'll play.

—Bernie Reagan

Snakes? They're bad. They'll bite you. They're poison, snakes. There's rattlesnakes, there's water moccasins, there's green snakes. They're all bad. A water moccasin has teeth and they'll bite you. A rattlesnake has teeth too and they'll bite you, they'll poison you. They curl up and they snap at you. A green snake isn't poisonous. They can grow on your lawn. But they spit at you and they'll give you a rash and if they spit in your eye you'll go blind. That's why they spit at flies, that's how they catch flies. They coil up and they spit at flies and beetles and insects.

—Andrew Legrice

A snake is a, well, a, like, a snake is like a fish. It's in the animal world. It crawls like an animal. A snake is poison. It's like a, whaddyacallit, it crawls. I know it crawls, it crawls anyway. It crawls on the ground. You don't see too many snakes around here, though.

—*Ed Rogers*

They're dangerous. They live in the ground. At times they can creep. They twist and crawl. The body has to twist to move. If the body was straight it couldn't move, could it? There's a large variety of snakes. A large variety of birds also. And animals. A large variety of animals and birds. There's also a large variety of buildings and furniture. And flowers . . . ships . . . and radio and television . . . also jewelry, a large variety of jewelry.

—*Ernie Brookings*

Frank Kanslasky: Fish got a heart?

DG: Yes.

Frank: No he ain't, fish ain't got no heart.

Andy Legrice: What do they have?

Frank: I don't know, but no heart.

Andy: How the hell do they breathe?

Frank: Like fish.

Bill LaGasse: Gills.

Andy: Gills, that's their heart.

Frank: Gills?! I don't know where their heart is. I don't think they even got a liver. Ever seen fish livers?

Bernie Reagan: Yeah.

I'm sorry, fish and me don't agree. I don't know. Fish and me don't agree—they're on one side of the street and I'm on the other, five blocks away. *Ken Eglin*

I don't know, I only eat them, I don't work on fish. *Bill LaGasse*

They have no sex life. *Gil Greene*

I don't like fish, I always get hamburger. *John Fay*

Well, they usually have to have water to live in, 'cause it's bad to see when a water hole, or wherever they are, dries up and they're flappin' around and they'll probably die because they're not able to breathe too well on land—they have to have water to breathe, don't they? And good fish is supposed to be a good source or supply for your brain, so your brain will grow and you can keep your energy up, so you'll be able to function properly, and you might even be able to think better and everything. *Bill Niemi*

Fish swim, they travel in schools. And, ah, I had a fishin' rod and I used to go fishin' all the time. Some rods I rented, some I bought. *Bernie Reagan*

I don't know, I'm not in the fisherman's union. They have gills, they have fins and gills, that's all I know about fishin'. (*Sings*) Well I'm a-goin' fishin', there's a smile upon my face, goin' fishin'—I don't know the rest of the words of the song, that's all I know. (*Sings*) Well it's only a paper moon, sailing under a cardboard sky, but it wouldn't be make-believe if you believed in me. (*DG: Thank you.*) There's more, that's not the whole song. (*Sings*) Oh it's a love, love, love, oh it's a honky-tonk parade, oh it's a melody played in a penny arcade, for it's a Barnum and Bailey world, just as phony as it can be, but it wouldn't be make-believe if you believed in me. (*DG: Thank you.*) You're welcome, Dave. I'm waiting for my dinner. Time is going by. Time waits for no one. The essence of time. (*Walks away, singing*) Well, it's only a paper moon…*Jack Mudurian*

FRANK: You did? Where?

BERNIE: In the fish market.

FRANK: I don't think so.

BERNIE: He said, "I got some fish livers, I want you to take some with you." He gave me a whole carton.

FRANK: Yeah, I think they were chicken livers.

ANDY: Could be. I haven't heard of 'em, fish livers.

FRANK: Do fish let out waste, like people?

ANDY: Yeah.

FRANK: They do?

BILL: Where they get perfume from.

ANDY: Ambergris.

FRANK: From whales. They've got to throw up, though. . . . If he ain't got no liver then he can't go to the bathroom, right? You've got to have a liver, right?

BILL: They go to the bathroom.

ANDY: They wag their tails and let it go, in the ocean.

FRANK: I don't think so.

ANDY: Where do they go then?

FRANK: What do you mean, "Wagging his tail"? His tail is just to guide him, like a boat, a ship. If they didn't have a tail they wouldn't be able to steer.

BERNIE: They had a diving bell.

DG: Who did?

BERNIE: The navy. They let you down to go down to the floor of the ocean and the fish would enter it.

ANDY: No, the fish don't enter the diving bell, you go down to *see* the fish.

BILL: The people are in there. Sure, they explore the bottom of the ocean with it. They designed it to find sunken ships.

DAVID BREWER: (*Shakes his head*) They just designed the diving bell to go down and to find how to live down there. And now they can't live down there, that's why they're going into outer space. And they can't live up there, either.

FRANK: Oh sure they will, eventually they will. They'll get rid of their lungs and they'll live. As long as you got no lungs you're all right—you got lungs, you'll die.

ANDY: Oooooooh! If you don't have lungs you'll die. That's what makes your heart pump.

FRANK: Do birds have lungs?

ERNIE BROOKINGS: Aren't lungs necessary for breathing?

FRANK: For a bird, I don't know.

ERNIE: I think so.

FRANK: I don't know, I just asked.

BERNIE: They have a gizzard.

ERNIE: Too many kinds of birds.

FRANK: Sure, there's too many kinds of birds.

ERNIE: Ostriches, robins, hawks and seagulls. And pelicans. Pheasants. Sparrows and robins and bluebirds.

FRANK: I s'pose they're all around havin' a good time.

ERNIE: Crows and hawks and seagulls. And eagles.

FRANK: They're nasty bastards.

ERNIE: Eagles—the national bird of the United States.

FRANK: They're terrible, just like a hawk.

ERNIE: Another kind is hens.

ANDY: Crows.

ERNIE: Peacocks and woodpeckers, right?

Can roaches be trained?

ABE SURGECOFF: They can be trained in a certain way, like hive and honey, just like that.

JOHN LOWTHERS: It all depends. Throw a little bread around and they'll come right after it.

GEORGE STINGEL: No, I don't think so, they're insects.

JIM THIEBEDEAU: It don't seem possible to me.

FERGIE: Cockroaches?

DG: Yes.

FERGIE: Yes.

DG: They can?

FERGIE: Certainly, by an electrical instrument.

WALTER KIERAN: I don't know, I'm not even interested.

DG: You're not?!

WALTER: Of course not! That's a foolish question to ask me.

WALTER MCGEORGE: I imagine so, every damned thing else is trained.

HAROLD FARRINGTON: They can be trained, just like any other insect or animal. Treat 'em good, feed 'em good, and they can be trained. And they'll bring their neighbors over if you have a good house.

FRANCIS MCELROY: Sure!

DG: How?

FRANCIS: By being taught by intelligent people.

FRANK KANSLASKY: Better go ask a roach.

BERNIE REAGAN: Roaches?

DG: Yes.

BERNIE: Be trained?

DG: Yes.

BERNIE: I don't know, I don't think so. . . . There was a hole one time in the wall and the roaches kept comin' out of it.

BILL NIEMI: Roaches? (*DG: Yes.*) You'd have to be crazy to train roaches, wouldn't you—they bite and they crawl all over the place. They're very dirty vermin.

FRANK: Was there rats and mice way back? About 808.

ANDY: Oh, sure.

FRANK: I don't think so.

Ernie: Another bird is a crow. Crows and hawks, hawks and crows.

ANDY: There's always been rats and mice. Water rats, field mice, muskrats.

ERNIE: Bluebirds. And pigeons.

FRANK: (*Shakes his head*) There was none. There was no people so there was no rats and mice. When people became plentiful they made rats and mice.

ANDY: Waste food and the rats would live on the food they waste.

ERNIE: People would be jailbirds, if they're in jail.

ABE SURGECOFF: Rats and mice eat the wheat too.

FRANK: They'd eat you too—if they're hungry, I s'pose. They're particular, though, they like nice food, just like people. They like to live in houses, motels, hotels, apartments, ships—I don't know about airplanes. They like to live with people.

ERNIE: Another bird is doves, they're similar to pigeons. Aren't doves usually white?

FRANK: Any color they can become, I suppose. . . . A pigeon is a stoolie, ain't he? Right?

ERNIE: Could be.

LARRY GREEN: A stool pigeon.

ERNIE: A stool pigeon.

LARRY: Yeah.

ERNIE: Could be a person.

ABE: No. (*Shakes his head*)

FRANK: Sure we are, we're all stool pigeons. How else do you think we live?

ED: Do you believe that?

FRANK: Sure, we're all stool pigeons.

ERNIE: There's a bird in the arctic, I don't recall their name right now.

ED: There's different kinds of birds, different kinds, different types.

ERNIE: Otherwise there wouldn't be variety.

ED: Different kinds.

ABE: The mother hollers for the small chicks.

ERNIE: Essentially a large variety.

ABE: A fish is a stool pigeon too.

FRANK: A fish?! (*Laughs*) Oh, boy!

ED POINDEXTER: A fish is a stool pigeon.

DG: What do you mean?

ED P.: I don't know. May I have a cigarette?

FRANK: I don't think it is, why should he be?

ABE: A bigger fish eats a smaller fish.

FRANK: That's like here, they do the same thing here.

ERNIE: Admiral Perry discovered the North Pole; Admiral Byrd, the South Pole.

FRANK: How could he discover it, it was there all the time.

ED R.: (*Laughs*)

ERNIE: I heard it direct by shortwave radio in Springfield, Vermont. I don't recall the date.

ED P.: Cookout?

DG: It's raining.

JACK MUDURIAN: Kill them with your foot. (*DG: What about training?*) Can't train them, they're too small to be trained.

ED POINDEXTER: No, nothing you can do with them. Down at the sugar refinery, they'd go like a wild bug. You spray some cockroach killer and they go wild. They've got a nest of small ones, and then they get big. And the big ones make small ones.

dp

DG: Do apes have picnics?

ERNIE BROOKINGS: I don't know, my dictionary's too small.

dp

KEN EGLIN: You ever hear that saying, "Elephants never forget?" Well, it's a lot of shit—elephants forget the same as everyone else

dp

I was home alone and saw an ant on the floor and went after it. And as I went after it with my foot it kept going away and finally it went through the kitchen door into the vestibule. There's a step there and I went down it and I got down on my knees, trying to catch the ant, it was going away. And then I couldn't get up off my knees and I was right at the top of the stairs and I was afraid of falling down them. I had to lay there and wait for my husband to come home. When he saw me, he was carrying some bundles and he just dropped them, and he came right over to me. I was all shook up, but I was alright, I didn't fall.

So now when I see an ant I just let it run, I don't follow it. *Ann Stark*

ERNIE: A butterfly is not a bird. A flying insect is a butterfly.

ABE: No.

ERNIE: No, too small.

HAROLD FARRINGTON: Do they have an oleo-fly?

FRANK: Nabisco!

ERNIE: Another bird is the oriole.

HAROLD: You've got Admiral Byrd, too.

FERGIE: Admiral Leahy. L-E-A-H-Y.

DG: Who's he?

FERGIE: One of the greatest admirals we ever had.

FRANK: Leahy? He must mean the guy at Notre Dame. He wasn't no admiral, though.

HAROLD: Frank Leahy.

FERGIE: Frank Leahy is right.

FRANK: He might have been in the navy.

FERGIE: He was. What's for lunch?

ABE: Fish.

FRANK: Now they're murdering fish, just like everything else.

HAROLD: Eddie Fischer.

FERGIE: What about him?

HAROLD: He's a crooner.

FRANK: He's a junkie. And a drunk.

HAROLD: He was married to—

FRANK: —Elizabeth Taylor.

FERGIE: Yes, and she's a millionairess. Alice Viola Fischer.

DG: Who's that?

FERGIE: Eddie Fischer's wife.

I can't complain too much,

I've been to California.

Ed Poindexter

Bill Niemi

Where in the world would you like a one-way ticket to?

ANTHONY ESPOSITO: One-way ticket? Geez, I don't know. Where would you go?

DG: New Zealand.

ANTHONY: New Zealand?

DG: Yeah.

ANTHONY: What are they gonna do, give a ticket away?

DG: No.

ANTHONY: Oh, that's yours.

DG: It's hypothetical.

ANTHONY: They're not givin' anything away! *(Laughs)*

DG: Where would you go?

ANTHONY: *(Laughs)* I don't know, I don't know where the hell I'd go. At my age it's kinda rough. Where would you go?

DG: New Zealand.

ANTHONY: New Zealand—you ever been out there?

DG: No, it's pretty far away.

I traveled up to Washington, D.C.—that's about 4,000 miles, I think it's 4,000 miles. And I came there and went to Europa, that's a city in Washington, D.C.—a small town. That's the state of Washington, don't forget it's the state of Washington. And they found the people up there less hospitality. And when I was up there they had the 8th Air Force and, ah, some of the families didn't want to walk on the same side of the street as the soldiers. I went to buy some stuff there and the people jacked up the price. And we went in to have a beer and beer was high for the non-coms—they didn't like the non-coms. And, ah, we went to the movies out there and we found out they was non-hospitality too. Let's see now . . . let's see now . . . the food out there was awful expensive to eat out there. The Red Cross was not for some of the soldiers there, the non-coms. Let's see . . . they had nice homes out there and some of the non-coms were treated with kindness. Some of them would call out to the neighbors in the non-com section. The soldiers would come and they had their own way of spendin' money.

We went down on the train as far as New York and the food was not too excellent to eat on the train. And when we'd stop the people would say to go ahead, don't stop there—we were going through their fields. We had to load water in the engine. We found out from the people that there were big snakes that jumped at least ten foot high. We rode by another place and it was less dangerous, but we couldn't get off the train till when the engine was startin' goin'.

—Abe Surgecoff

I like New York—I've been there nine times. It's fascinating, it is, I think it's great. I went to the U.N. every time I went except the last time. I like Yonkers, that's where my sister-in-law lives.

But if they're gonna sell Tylenol there I'm not goin'—that's where that woman lived who died from Tylenol!

But I really do like New York. We stayed at the Times Square Hotel and we stayed at the Plymouth Hotel. We went to the Statue of Liberty and went up the Empire State Building and we walked past Madison Square Garden and I touched the door. Somebody said, "Isn't that Madison Square Garden?" And my minister said, "Why, yes it is." And I said, "Oh wow, I want to go in!" And he said, "Well there's nothing going on in there now." And I said, "Well I want to at least touch the door, I don't think they'll mind that." And I went over and laid my own hand right on the door!

And we went to Radio City Music Hall. A hundred dancing girls all doing the same thing, that's really something! And what legs! They've all got pretty faces too. Those geezers are terrific! And in the same place I saw a movie of Cary Grant. Some bad guys were chasing him all over the presidents' faces on Mount Rushmore. I like Cary, he's nice.

—Daphne Matthews

Travel? All over Europe. England, Europe, Scotland, New Germany, South America, Tierra del Fuego, the Straits of Gibraltar and this country. I was in Kentucky and Tennessee, Florida, Washington state, Washington, D.C. Nova Scotia was my favorite place to go. My wife's parents lived there. It's nice. Go fishing. I bought a fishin' rod at Sears and Roebuck in North Cambridge and went fishing. Nine Mile Lake. And I went fishin' with Burke—I worked for Burke Engineering. I took the trips down on the fishin' boat. And *Queen Mary* and *Queen Elizabeth;* I was workin' on them in the yard. We put elevators in there, made elevators. Otis Elevator Company.

—Bernie Reagan

ANTHONY: I haven't been anywhere.

DG: So, where would you want to go?

ANTHONY: I don't know. I've been to Florida.

BERNICE MOROS: Well you've been somewhere, then, I haven't been to Florida.

ANTHONY: I took a trip there once.

BERNICE: You ever watch that Dating Game? They take you to nice places.

ANTHONY: Dating Game?

BERNICE: Yeah, the girl picks a man and they send them on nice trips.

ANTHONY: What channel is that on?

BERNICE: Channel ten, seven o'clock. I like it.

DG: You gonna watch it?

ANTHONY: The Dating Game?

BERNICE: It's interesting and all the fellas are dressed so nice. Suits and ties.

I gave up driving. Over seventy-two years of driving and nobody hurt, so it's a good time to stop. What's going on nowadays, you never can tell. Just stay out of the bars. *Neil Henderson*

I keep smokin', but what I really want to do is drive around in a stick-shift car. I'd drive my mother to Nantasket Beach. *Jack Mudurian*

If you leave your car outside on a cold night it'll eat up a gallon of gas in a half hour. *Herbie Caldwell*

It's just my wife and I. I didn't travel anywhere special. I'm a great worker—I mean walker, rather. I walked from the bottom of Tremont Street—that's Tremont and Court Street—all the way to Ashmont Station. I like to walk.

When I got married, I spent a honeymoon in New York—New York City. I like New York City. I like to walk. And my brother-in-law—he's dead now—he worked for the Chase National Bank in New York. . . . That's where I spent my honeymoon is in New York.

I was an air raid warden in Boston here. I worked in the Copley Plaza and I worked in the Hotel Statler—that's right in Park Square there. I ran the elevators there. And I worked in Plant Shoes Company in Jamaica Plain—Thomas G. Plant. . . . What else? . . . um . . . oh, yeah! I was a laborer in the state highway. It was a year appointment I had.

—Frances McElroy

I've been to Maine two or three times. China, Maine—just like the main country of China. It's eight miles from Waterville. Spent a few weeks with a friend of mine who had relatives down there. They had a sailboat, went out in that a few times with him. Just a regular vacation—taking it easy, laying around. We went to a church supper down there, that was a good time.

—George MacWilliams

dp

I traveled all over the country but I never made it to California, and I could kick myself.

Colorado's a nice state, they have mountains there and everything.

I never got to California, I could kick myself. I never got there—I could've, but I didn't—I stopped before I got there.

I lived in Nebraska for seven years with my aunt. I lived in Tamorah, thirty-two miles from Lincoln. That's a great place, Lincoln. I used to go up and see my cousins in Lincoln.

I went to Chicago, the toddling town they used to call it, but I don't know why. I left it when my father sent for me and I came back, to the greatest town in the world—New York. And it *is* the greatest town in the world, in my estimation.

—*Edna Hemion*

My favorite trip I took was when I was in the service. I went overseas to Italy. I seen a lot of villages that I had read on a map here in the states, that I never thought I'd ever see. And I'll tell you the God's truth: American people, they say "Rome"—it's not Rome, it's Rom*a*—it's not pronounced Rome it's Rom*a*. How you spell it, I don't know—it's Roma—there's an "a" at the end of it, I know. When you're there you can find out the correct pronunciation of different things. I knew about Pisa, Viareggio, Forte dei Marmi—I knew all that—but I was surprised to know that I was sleeping right outside the Pisa on the ground—the Pisa—the Leaning Tower—I almost shit!

I went all over Italy—I can't pronounce all the names of it—from Naples right to the end. I was in Pole Valley when we got

I never owned a car, I was too nervous. My mother wouldn't let me learn to drive. I was trying to learn to drive a car once—I got it started but I didn't know how to stop it. I went down the ramp on Storrow Drive and came down to the bottom and hit some big rocks and they stopped the car, so I turned the key and turned it off. The M.D.C. police came and said, "Hey, what are you doing? You can't drive!" I said, "I know, I'm trying to learn." And they said, "Where's the other fellow who's supposed to be with you?" "He went to get help," I told them.

Yep, those rocks stopped me; they saved me from going right in to the Charles. I'd've gone right into the Charles River and gone right to the bottom.

So I never learned to drive—I almost killed myself that time.

Ken Eglin

Even if I had been a driver I tell myself that I wouldn't be driving by now anyway. That's my consolation.
Sophie Terkel

Massachusetts is one of the greatest shoe states in the country. Especially ladies' shoes. They have ladies' shoes that go right up to your knee—and I mean up to your knee. And they didn't used to have much on. And when they'd lace those babies up you could see from here to Winston Churchill, and you know what a tall son-of-a-bitch he was. And they'd fall down and say it was their equilibrium—ha! Equilibrium my ass! Those decks were slippery as a cake of ice and we went to the South Pole. Chrissake—it was freezing down there! They were lucky if they had a coal stove. *Fergie*

word that President Roosevelt died, and that Harry Truman was our new commanding officer. The Great Harry. I always call him the Great Harry because he was so-o-o-o . . . I can't describe it the way I want to. I have respect for that man, I have a lot of respect for him in a lot of ways. Two things: if he wanted to say "damn" or "hell" he would say it. Those two things, that's what I'd prize him for. The only other president I knew who'd say that—I wasn't around then, neither were you—Roosevelt, Teddy Roosevelt. He'd swear like a bitch! He'd swear up a trooper! I read that. I think that's the reason why he didn't get reelected—he was too tough.

—Ken Eglin

I went to Chicago half a dozen times. That was around 1940. Just vacations. I had friends there. There's so much about Chicago, so much that's good. That's why they call it the Magic City. So much for the good. I settled there after I'd visited. I worked on the railroad. I'm from Virginia originally. Chicago's a city that everything happens in—places to go, things to do. I guess that's why they rightfully call it the Magic City. Nothin's out of reach with a little effort. It's the kind of city you dream about. I also like its sister state, Indiana. In Chicago you can make something new happen everyday. I miss Chicago, I do. I miss Chicago very much. Chicago's a city where you always find something to do. That's why we call it the Never Lonely City. Oh, I could sit here all day and talk about Chicago, but I know you don't have that kind of time on your hands. Want to wrap it up? (*DG: How do we do that?*) I'd just say that a lot of people call Chicago the Magic City—I call it the City That Never Sleeps.

—Walter McGeorge

I've been many places in my lifetime. What would you like to know? (*DG: What was your favorite trip?*) Ah . . . Paris. Or was it the White Mountains? Where else . . . I wish I was in Germany, I wish I stayed there. The hills of Tennessee . . . the Mohawk Trail. Ever heard of it? At the bottom of the Mohawk Trail there's a souvenir store and you stop in and buy all kinds of trinkets. They've got pillowcases with a picture of the Mohawk Trail on it. Very nice. Fringe on the ends.

I took a lot of pictures because wherever I went I'd take my camera. I had three albums filled with pictures. I often wonder if they're still around. I used to reminisce a lot because I had a lot to reminisce about, and I'd take out the photo albums. You know, pictures of old friends. My army days in Germany. Did I have fun in Germany! Fraternizing with German girls . . . oooh, she loved me! Every night I used to go and see her . . . they're all dead now and nothing I can do about it. I'm lucky to be alive.

—*Frank Wisnewski*

I never traveled. I never took a trip. I went to New York, but that ain't a trip, it's an adventure. New York is old time. I went there quite a few times. Used to stay at the Saloon House, eat there too. I'd go to the show—walk up to the show. It was a mile away. I didn't drink in New York. My brother lived there and I didn't want to cause no ill feelings. I'd worry him to death. He's a good guy but he doesn't want me in jail from drinking. Of course I was old enough, but I didn't want to get him in no trouble. I was picked up on a vagrancy charge by a policeman and the judge let me go and I went back to where I was staying. I was broke. I guess they called my brother but he didn't show. They let me go anyhow. Told them I was broke and gettin' out of town. I was gonna get out of town as soon as I could get my

FERGIE: Niagara Falls—the finest falls there are in the world. Up and down. It's a beautiful, beautiful scene, one of the most gorgeous scenes you ever looked at. Boys and girls around here, that you know around here very well, have gone up the falls and down the falls and up and down, and they're still going up and down the greatest falls in the world. The water goes straight up and it comes straight down. You know who controls it?

DG: Who?

FERGIE: The Lord Jesus Christ. Capital J-E-S-U-S, capital C-H-R-I-S-T.

DG: How did he get in charge of the falls?

FERGIE: Because he's in charge of everything. He's in charge of the world. He can fly over the falls, he can go up or he can come down. If you have any more questions to ask, you ask him. But be sure you have an army with you when you ask him.

Niagara Falls—one of the most beautiful spots in the world. If you can fly, you can fly there. You can go anywhere you want.

I don't want a car right now. I slept pretty good last night, but I'm not ready to drive a car. *Henry Turner*

bearings. Find my whereabouts. When I found my bearings I left for home—Newport, Rhode Island. I took to the road and was glad to get out of that measly town.

—Bill LaGasse

We are all sweethearts—some of us are fresh sweethearts and some of us are stale.

Fergie

Abe Surgecoff

Did you ever have a perfect kiss?

I think the nicest kiss I got was from Muhammed Ali. *Jeanne Malone*

No, not for a long time I ain't had one. I'm not the master. Some of 'em say, "You're the master." Nope, I ain't the master—no way! *Viljo Lehto*

I been kissed by a lot of females, when I say goodnight to them, after the date's over with. (*DG: Were any of them perfect kisses?*) Just a kiss. *Wallace Baker*

Never! How the hell do I know what a perfect one is!? *John Hodorowski*

A *perfect* one? I don't know what a perfect one is—I've had a lot of 'em, though. You ask a girl, "What shape is a kiss? Give me one and we'll call it square!" (*Laughs*) *Roy Elliott*

Did you ever have a broken heart?

Yeah, I had one. Can't say much. A girlfriend or somethin'. I had a date with her and she run off and leave me, I guess. Rosie Speares of Danvers. She looked pretty good, she looked good. We used to go out nights. We'd go to Salem or something. I used to give her presents, a ring or something, I guess. Chocolates and flowers—pinks or something, I guess. It was a pretty good year. We'd go sportin'. Yeah, I had broken hearts. I lost my mother two years ago—that's a broken heart. Got me knocked out.

—*Herbie Caldwell*

No, I never had time for that. I was too busy, too busy. People, they get broken hearts and that's all they think of—they don't think of anything else. I was too busy with a lot of girls. Too busy for broken hearts. Variety is the spice of life. Why tie yourself down to one when you can be free and love 'em all. And I never hurt any of them—I was too easy with 'em. I made friends and I kept 'em. I didn't lose 'em doing something foolish. They all liked me because I was good to 'em. I never saw more than one at a time. Just one at a time. I didn't rush 'em off their feet; I'd take my time with 'em—I didn't rush 'em. I got more lovin' that way, if you don't rush 'em. A man makes a mistake when he rushes and hurries a woman; he don't get any love out of 'em. They don't want to give him any love. I wish good luck to everybody, to everybody I come in contact with.

—*Walter Kieran*

No, never had a broken heart. I never had anything like that happen to me. Everything went smooth. Just luck, I guess. She used to buy meat in Grant's and bring it home and cook it. She was a good cook. Got along fine. We still do. She's working for Grant's. She's gonna be retired pretty soon. We got along fine. She didn't approve of me talkin' to other women, except relatives of hers. She'd ask me, "What does she want?" she'd say, if she saw me talkin' to a woman.

—*Bernie Reagan*

My heart just wasn't born with a will to succeed. That's about my life story.

—*Warner Day*

When I lost my mother. I didn't give a damn anymore. Started drinkin' and runnin' around with girls. I just didn't care. No girl ever broke my heart, though—you know me better than that. No girl could ever break my heart. They can break all these people's hearts, but they ain't break mine. I'll never tell any girl I love her—I'll never tell that to any girl in my life. Only my mother. I don't know what love is. They say to me, "I love her," and I say, "Okay, get married. Enjoy yourself." And three months later they're in court for a divorce and I'm sittin' there listening and laughing, and they say, "Kenny, you were right." Honest to God, all my life I could never see a guy sayin' "I love you" to a girl. They say, "Kenny, you want to come with us on a date?" and I just go down to the beach, down to the Charles River. And down at Magazine Beach, I see guys sayin' to girls, "I love you," and I say, "You damn fools."

—*Ken Eglin*

FERGIE: The last time my mother went and gave me all her money. One hundred million dollars. Did you hear that? One hundred million dollars she gave me. And you know what I did with it? I put it in the First National Bank. F-I-R-S-T National Bank. One hundred million dollars.

DG: What's that have to do with a broken heart?

FERGIE: Well, it kind of takes care of it monetarily. You know what I mean, monetarily? They asked me what I would do and I told them: I would take one hundred grand out of the First National and put it in the Shawmut. You know, the First

I don't know what that is. I used to have a tool kit. I used to keep my tools in a dinner box, or in a drawer. They're all gone now, gave 'em away. Pliers, socket wrenches, I used to have everything. *Fred Delap*

I think it's almost impossible to get anything perfect. *Eddie Rutter*

Jesus Christ! I don't know! I probably did, probably did. *John Bitowski*

Kind of a personal question, isn't it? *Alice Bitowski*

Of course! *Daphne Matthews*

Yeah, blissful kiss. *George Vrooman*

If your wife was over here, I'd kiss her. Would that make you mad? *Viljo Lehto*

No! (*Laughs*)—yeah, I'll have to answer yes, once. That's a good question. *Bill Hughes*

A perfect kiss? Yes. And the woman warned me before she kissed me. She said, "After I kiss you you're gonna go wild and wanna take me to bed, but alls you can do is kiss me." And she was right. *Joe Ciarciaglino*

Sure, my wife. *Larry Green*

No, not really. Who would you get that from these days? Probably Santa Claus. *Bill Niemi*

FRANK KANSLASKY: See you later.

GENE EDWARDS: Ha! Ha! See you later! Don't you write that down!

FRANK: Yeah, write that down.

No, that's out of my field. *Bill LaGasse*

Don't swear. *Pasquale Troiano*

If a pretty girl let me kiss her I'd take her for a ride in the car, if I had a car to drive. *Jack Mudurian*

Yeah, I think I did. *John Fallon*

BOB SHIREY: What constitutes a perfect kiss?

DAPHNE MATTHEWS: A woman, I suppose.

BOB: Absolute involvement and, ah—

BILL HUGHES: Fidelity.

BOB: No, no, that has nothing to do with fidelity.

BILL: Well, it could have.

BOB: Uncompromising commitment to the act of kissing.

National is one of the largest banks in the world, and the Shawmut National isn't too far behind. They've got one hundred million too. Not two hundred million, one hundred million.

DG: Who broke your heart?

FERGIE: My mother. She said, "What are you going to do with a hundred million dollars if I give it to you?" I said, "I'll spend it on you." And she said, "Well, go ahead and start spending." She said, "Where are you going to spend all this money?" And I said, "I'll spend it at Gilchrist's and Jordan Marsh and Filene's and Raymond's." And she said, "Raymond's! At that filthy rotten store?" It may be filthy dirty, but it's not filthy rotten, it's filthy rich. It's the richest store in the world. And everybody knows it.

I don't remember having one. No sweetheart troubles. I must have been born lucky.

—John Lowthers

Yeah, my wife. That's about all. It's a long story, Dave. I took my daughter to basketball games, the Globetrotter game, the hockey game, baseball. My wife, she just walked out the door. Took the kid too.

Another thing that broke my heart, I found my mother dead in bed. I was only a kid. I remember my mother takin' me to church. Holdin' my hand and goin' to church. She had a stroke

—John Fay

No, I don't think so. I was thinking about I used to write some songs. It was not a sweetheart, but it was a girl, and she sang a couple of my songs on television and also on radio. The songs were something about her and where she came from, she thought, so she started takin' a likin' to me. That's all. She was a nurse, a nurse at a hospital. She had to make up her mind about what I was doin' and she realized that I fell in love with somebody else. She was nice-looking and so forth and so on.

They both worked in the hospital. One worked in the Beth Israel Hospital and one was in Mass. General Hospital. They were both pretty. Have you got one? They wanted me to work in the hospital, which I refused to do. Once she realized that I loved someone else, she hesitated. There was a party and I met her at a party—she was there—they both were there. One nurse talking to another, they got so friendly and that's how they happened to find out. One did like it and one didn't like it. After a while they both disliked me for a while and I told 'em where to go.

She called me up from Beth Israel Hospital one time and she wanted me to take her out, but I didn't do it because I was just coming back from the service and involved with the family.

If this doesn't sound good to you, just tear it up.

—Abe Surgecoff

I've been married. It didn't work. That was years ago—army days. It passes away. I'm not repeating it. Baseball's the topic now.

—John Colton

Sometimes yes, sometimes no. It just breaks once in a while for various reasons. Different reasons'll do it—I'm not with the race horses. In one sense, not being where you want'll do it.

—Frank Hooker

Yeah, it's tough, I had a romance go sour. She left me. She didn't get mad, she just walked off. I don't know why. She went down to Nova Scotia. I haven't seen her for years. Her name is Dorothy. I think about her, about when I can see her.

—Larry Green

I guess so. I guess a lot of people have broken hearts. You know, bad things happen to them. I was put in a bad place for a while, you know. It wasn't a very nice place. I guess everybody

The old woman took notions and went out and kissed the cow. She kissed the cow because her husband wouldn't kiss her.

I used to hear stories like that when I was in the marines—in the marines-underneath-the-water. They used to talk awful. One guy said to me, "Get me a Budweiser!" I said, "Get you a Budweiser?! I ain't a bartender!" *Viljo Lehto*

Yeah, one girl, we went dancin' years ago and she grabbed me and kissed me all over. I still remember. *John Fay*

Well, I had a kiss but one had a bacteria mouth. That's why you go to the dentist, that's an important thing. *Abe Surgecoff*

Oh yeah, that's been many years ago, many years gone by. Twenty-two years ago. One kiss led to another and then that led us into bed. Hide the weenie! *Andy Legrice*

Yes I did, years ago. From my wife. I was married December fifteenth, 1928, in Burlington, Vermont. She was very efficient. Her name was Merta Elizabeth Monroe. *Ernie Brookings*

dp

Why do people kiss?

WALTER KIERAN: Well I don't know, it's the way they feel.

BILL LAGASSE: They're lovers.

DAVID BREWER: They're trying' to get next to a good thing.

ANDY LEGRICE: They love each other.

BILL: There's friendly kisses, there's married kisses, there's all kinds of kisses. The kiss I like best is the sexier kiss.

DAVID: Oh, you're gettin' on it now!

JOHN FALLON: Because they feel like it.

ABE SURGECOFF: For pleasure enjoyment.

LARRY GREEN: To go to bed! (*Laughs*)

CHARLES SHEA: Sign of affection.

BILL NIEMI: Well, probably because it's a show of friendship. An old friend kisses another old friend, or a boy kisses a girlfriend so they can have fun together.

ERNIE BROOKINGS: To show their affection, their mutual affection.

FRANCIS MCELROY: To relax.

has to have a taste of something bad. You can't have everything perfect in this world. You've got to have a taste of something bad sometime so you know what it's like. I know I had one. Mine lasted a year.

—*Gene Edwards*

What the hell, I don't know anything about broken hearts. I came through everything as good as can be expected. No problems. All the wrongdoings I had done to me I had asked for. Everybody's free of mind, free of body, free of spirit—they do as they please. Whatever they're doing might affect you, it might seem wrong, but it isn't wrong. The thing that wrongs you maybe doesn't wrong everybody. They should call it obstacles of life. A tragic encounter. If I had my life to live over, would I do it the same? It's hard to say. It's food for thought. You could regret something but go ahead and do the same thing over the very same way. I wonder have I neglected myself or have I neglected my life. I don't think so, though I probably have. But it's unregretful neglect.

—*Walter McGeorge*

How did you meet your wife?

I don't recall, it's been long since.

—*Ernie Brookings*

I met her on the avenue, on Massachusetts Avenue, and I said to her, "Are you married?" And she said no. And I said, "Well, let's get married and raise a family." And we did.

—*Fergie*

At a dance. We liked each other, so we got married.

—*Jim Thibedeau*

At a house party. We got well acquainted then, and finally the outcome of the whole thing was we were man and wife.

—*John Lowthers*

No, no, no, no, I don't go that far.

—*Abe Surgecoff*

At a dance. We dated, for three years. She's still alive. She's my wife.

—*Fred Freeman*

Met her at a party. We hit it off. Courted her for a couple years. She finally said yes, she married me. We had a good wedding, St. Stephen's Church in Lynn.

—*Larry Green*

I met her because I liked her. And I kept company with her. And I finally married her. Still livin' happy. I never cross her up, I never argue with her. Always happy. Life is too short to be sad.

—*Francis McElroy*

Oooooh! After school, I went to school with her. I met her at the yacht club and we went out on the harbor on a moonlight cruise. We got in late after the cruise. I went home and I seen her again the next day. And, ah, well, then we went datin' and then we wound up hitched—that's the true test. It worked out, twenty-one years. Then we separated.

—*Andy Legrice*

I met her in a Polish barroom. She proposed and I got married—she proposed, I didn't, she did. I got married on puppy

ERNIE: Their lips would come in contact—bodily contact to the lips by kissing.

FRANK KANSLASKY: They got nothin' else to do.

HENRY TURNER: Because it's fun! I like to kiss too! Nothing wrong with that. Do you know, when my father was alive he never let me kiss him on the cheek—not even my own father let me kiss him on the cheek, or even a hug. And I loved my father more than Jesus. And Jesus is the Christian word for God, so I loved my father more than God.

BOB SHIREY Well, I think for one reason, it's so easy. It's a very easy thing to do. And it's a positive gesture, it's not negative. Why do people give people the finger? Becuase it's easy and it communicates. But it's the other way around, it means the opposite.

And it doesn't cost anything. It's cheaper than flowers, isn't it?! (*Laughs*) Yeah!

BILL HUGHES: (*Opens eyes wide*) Gee! Well, it's a preliminary sex act, and to show affection. It doesn't have to end up in sex, but it does have a sexual connotation, no matter how clean or mild. That's a good question, David.

DAPHNE MATTHEWS: Excellent.

BILL: Very good question.

DG: Daphne, what do you say—why do people kiss?

DAPHNE: Ah, sometimes out of appreciation. Sometimes if you do something nice for a person they'll say, "Oh, you're the most wonderful person in the world!"—and they throw their arms around you and kiss you.

BILL: Very good, Daphne.

BARBARA KATZ: 'Cause it goes back to ancient time and because they're in love.

ROY ELLIOTT: It gives 'em somethin' to remember 'em by, don't it?

WALLACE BAKER: Well, they've been doin' it for millions of years—accordin' to the Holy Bible, they kissed then.

love. It didn't last too long. You heard of puppy love? There's a lot of that puppy love around.

—*Ed Andrszweski*

I met her down in the Marine Corps. Army base. Sonny Frazier introduced us. Of course, we started goin' together. Of course, we finally got married. Of course, we had fifteen boys and girls, who lived happily ever after. That's the end of it.

—*Bill LaGasse*

What's it like to be a bachelor all your life?

Wonderful. You're free, ain't ya? Free from trouble. Free and happy, which I wouldn't be, married.

—*Walter Kieran*

For when I was single, oh how my pockets did jingle. (*DG: You were never married, though.*) No, I was never married. But when I was down in Rhode Island I had Alice Baker as my partner. I wasn't grown up at the time, but I was the same size as a grown person, the same size as her. When I first seen her down there she was bigger than me, because I wan't grown up at that time. Alice Baker, she's a brunette—prettiest girl in the world, no girl in the world was as pretty as her. If you'd look at her legs you'd agree with me on that.

—*Jack Mudurian*

Lousy. Don't ask me why, it's just lousy, that's all. No satisfaction. You know what I mean?

—*Charles Shea*

Well, you better make sure you have some good friends, besides bein' a bachelor. Bein' a bachelor means havin' more money for yourself, doesn't it? Room rents have gone up, haven't they? Taxation and everything's goin' up. And you have to pay what they want because roomin' houses need money too. Sometimes people have so much money they pay 'em way ahead of time, so they know you'll be welcome there later.

—Leo Germino

I'd rather be married. You won't be lonesome if you have a mate. I haven't seen my wife for forty-four years now.

—Harry Katz

(*Laughs*) Well, it's just the difference of bein' a bachelor is you're single. When you're single it's different from bein' married. You have more freedom. I mean, you're on your own, you're more free—you're single, that's all. That's the only difference—you're single, that's all.

—Ed Rogers

Well, you're always by yourself. (*DG: Is that good?*) No, that ain't too good.

—Bill LaGasse

WALTER MCGEORGE: I don't know how to answer that.

DG: Has it been good?

WALTER: Not exceptionally.

DG: Has it been bad?

WALTER: Just so-so.

I can't explain it myself, but I have been a bachelor all my life, that's all I do know.

—Edgar Major

VILJO LEHTO: That's for their love affair. They're startin' in on nature, you know, human nature.

JOHN HODOROWSKI: That, nobody answered me correctly, so I don't ask no more. See how the other side feels.

EARL WHITNEY: For a thrill, when you're havin' a sex attack. You know you kiss too because you're in love, you known that, don't you?

HOMER LAVIOLETTE: I don't know. The Eskimos rub noses, right? It's a custom probably thousands of years old. There's a lot of different kinds of kisses. Family relation kisses. In Arabian nations men kiss. A lot of things we look down on, like American men don't dance together, but they do in Arabian countries.

What's more important, romance or food?

CAMILLE PATRICK: Food!

RUTH LUBRANO: How can you be romantic without food?

SYBIL ROBERTSON: Food is one of the most basic necessities of life.

RUTH: And the other is necessary *for* life.

JANETTE LITTLE: Food.

ELMER WALLACH: You can get along without romance, you can't get along without food. That's my opinion now, don't quote me—oh, you're gonna quote me. I got along without romance, I'm still around.

CAMILLE: When you ask somebody in their seventies they're gonna say food.

ANNE RAPP: At our age I think food is more important than romance. At any age.

RUTH: When you're starving you're not gonna make love.

dp

What makes a good relationship?

Honesty, kindness, trust and, ah, bein' understanding. I guess that's about it.

—*Henry Turner*

Good partner.

—*Charles Shea*

Friends.

—*John Fay*

It would have to be a good friend, I guess. Someone who helps you, someone you can depend on. I haven't found that yet.

—*Gene Edwards*

Understanding.

—*Larry Green*

Happiness and coordination.

—*Ernie Brookings*

Doin' for 'em and help each other out. And, ah, divide the money. And, ah, lendin' clothes.

—*Abe Surgecoff*

Stay put in one place and stop movin' around unnecessarily.

—*Jack Mudurian*

Relationship—that means that you know the person that you're stayin' with. (*DG: What makes a good one?*) When you can be trustworthy with each other.

—*Leo Germino*

Marriage.

—George Stingel

Anything—friendship.

—John Fallon

Love, faith, honesty—that's everything.

—Andy Legrice

Companionship, or it could be by inheritance.

—Ernie Brookings

Minding your own business.

—Walter Kieran

Good behavior.

—Francis McElroy

Honesty.

—George Vrooman

Two people, a man and woman, my wife and me.

—Larry Green

Bein' by yourself—who knows?—do you know? I don't know. I s'pose each one holdin' a gun. How the hell do I know what makes a good relationship? Maybe one husband and three wives or one wife and three husbands—I don't know.

—Frank Kanslasky

ELMER: You don't need food when you have romance—when you have romance who thinks of food?

JOHN FAY: To me, I want to put some pounds on—food. Although I eat everything on the tray, I never gain a pound.

ANDY LEGRICE: Romance—oh yeah, you've got to have that, then you get the food afterwards.

ED ROGERS: Well, I think you have to have, ah, you need, I think food is the most important. You have to have food to keep your body going. Oh, romance is okay too, if you find someone you like. But on food, everyone has to have food for your body.

We hate each other's parting.
Abe Surgecoff

dp

Roseland, it's a classy dance place. I don't even know whether it's still in business or not. It's nice, very nice. They're strict there too—you have to behave yourself, you can't start any funny business. I don't even know if it's still in business or not. And I met my husband there. But he didn't dance—funny, huh? He tried, but he really wasn't much of a dancer. (*DG: What was the first thing he said to you?*) Oh, I can't remember that. Maybe, "Can I have this dance?" But he didn't dance much. Is it still in business? My dancing days are over 'cause my feet are bad.

—*Edna Hemion*

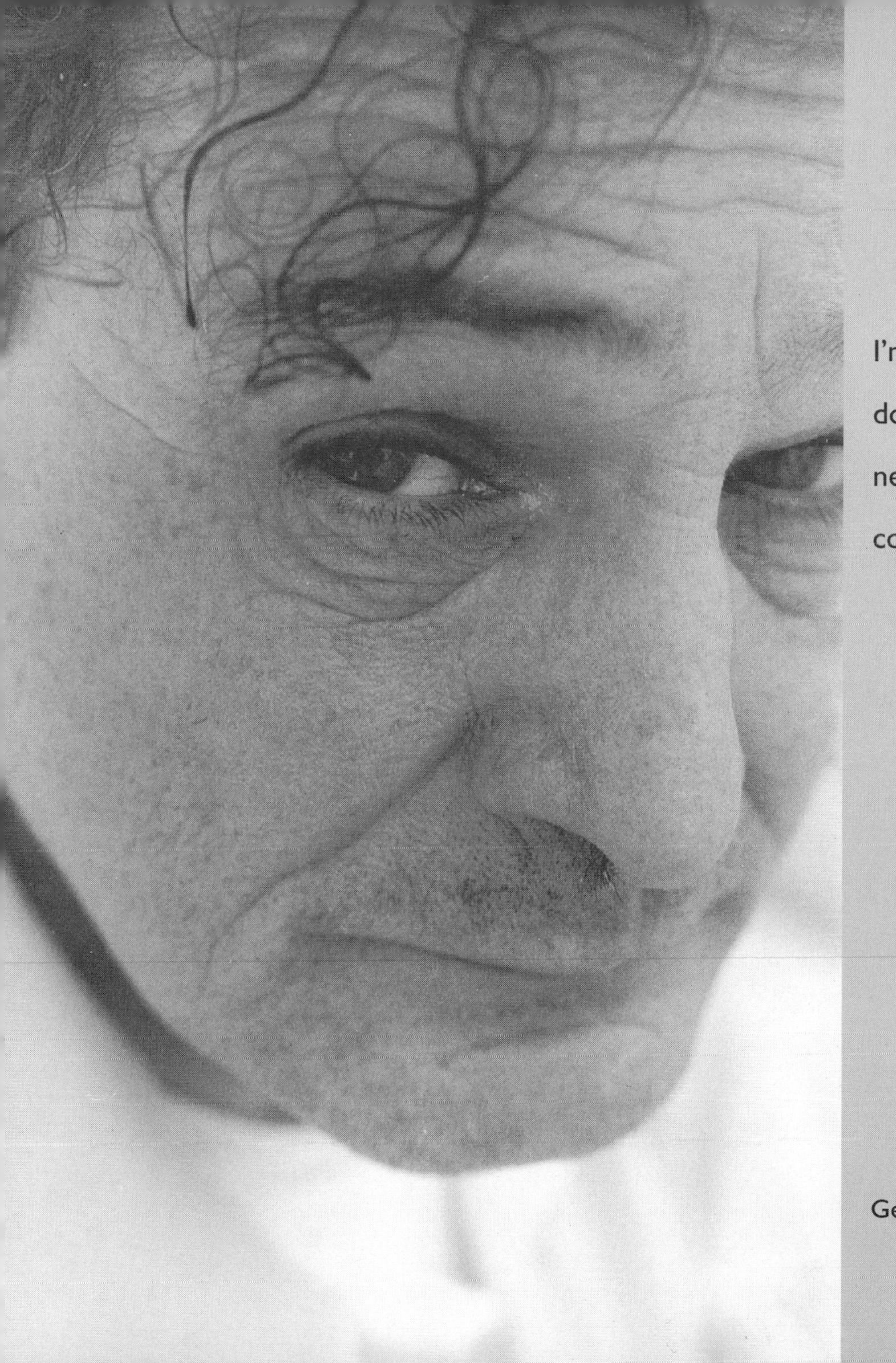

I'm supposed to drink, but I don't get a chance to. The nearest I can get to beer is coffee, I guess.

Herbie Caldwell

George Stingel

Would you swim in coffee if it wasn't too hot?

Yessss, I would. You want to know my Social Security number? *Ed Poindexter*

Well, I don't know, it depends on if it was sweetened up enough. *John Lowthers*

You get in there first and then I'll follow you. If you come out all right, then I'll come out all right. If you don't make it, then I ain't gonna make it, I ain't goin' in there either. *Frank Kanslasky*

I'd swim in anything if it wasn't too hot. *Fergie*

No, you don't swim in coffee, you drink it! Where do you live?! You put cream in it. *Andy Legrice*

No, because I can't swim. *Ernie Brookings*

You know what I say: All nuts don't come in shells! *Francis McElroy*

Coffee? It's all right. It's better than beer, or liquor. I have it just once a day, in the morning. I have soda the rest of the day. I don't have tea, I haven't had it since before they had it in tea bags. I used to like the tea that you could steep.

—Stan Abel

I'm not a coffee drinker. I just have one, and sometimes two, that's all, because I'm not a coffee drinker. Two cups a day. I take tea at night. Coffee I just have in the morning or at noon when it comes around, unless I don't feel like it.

—Margaret King

It's not good for you. I drink it, but I shouldn't.

—Edna Makely

It's no good for you, especially me, I have high blood pressure. I try to drink decaffeinated, at home I always do. It's not good for your nerves. I'm one of these jittery types, just like my mom.

—Bernice Moros

ANTHONY ESPOSITO: I like it! (*Laughs*) I like coffee, I don't know what else. I like food.

DG: Yeah, I like food, too.

ANTHONY: (*Laughs*)

I like coffee. I try not to drink too much because there's a lot of caffeine in it, which I don't need. But if I limit myself to four cups a day I'm okay. I suppose I could do without it, but I like it and I don't know as it hurts me, at least I don't see any side effects.

—Leona Quant

You know, some people take a cup and they don't put money in—that's a damn shame!

—John Catrambone

I drink it, but I can take it or leave it.

—*Ann Stark*

I couldn't drink if for a long, long time. But now I do. And I drink it black. If I put the milk or sugar in it, it turns me off.

—*Janette Little*

They make a good cup of coffee—that's good for them to know, that's true—they make a nice cup of coffee here.

—*Anne Stuart*

JOHN FAY: I can't drink enough of it.

ANDY LEGRICE: It's good for you.

JOHN: I'd rather have coffec than any other stuff I drank.

ANDY: Better than liquor. You don't get drunk.

JOHN: Yeah, you can't get drunk on liquor.

ANDY: Coffee.

JOHN: Yeah, coffee, not liquor, I'm sorry. Too much is not good for you.

ANDY: Caffeine.

JOHN: Then you have that other kind, that's okay.

ANDY: Caffeine, nicotine, gasoline!

JOHN: (*Laughs*)

Sometimes I drink three cups a day. It gives me a lift. It gives me the spirit, it does something to me. I drink mostly instant coffee.

—*Herman Seftel*

It is very good, coffee, but I like it not much, coffee. One cup on the morning.

—*Rae Daynouska*

No, I don't know, I've got a headache anyhow. Somebody else'll answer it. *Ed Andrszweski*

No, that isn't good, to swim in coffee. It would stain your body all brown. *Bill Niemi*

Yes, I'd swim in coffee if it wasn't too hot, but the trouble is, it's too hot. And expensive. *Ed Poindexter*

No, I drink it! *(Laughs) George Stingel*

dp

Lookin' over the grounds, piece of strip land. It don't look too good. Can't grow coffee on it, we don't want it. *Bill LaGasse*

dp

See if there's a rich widow downstairs with a jar of coffee, will you? *Robert Cleaves*

dp

DG: Which came first, coffee or tea?

WALTER KIERAN: I say coffee, 'cause coffee is the biggest seller.

LEO GERMINO: The biggest seller is hot chocolate, it will be in the wintertime.

FRANCIS MCELROY: And half of the world is wacky, I tell 'em right to their kisser!

LEO: If you drink too much hot chocolate it moves your bowels. It moves *my* bowels, two doses of it does.

FRANCIS: And if you drink too much booze you're ready for the undertaker.

LEO: The trouble is, if you take a little liquor, if you have enough food in your stomach to mix with it, it'll absorb it.

ED ROGERS: If you drink too much beer it'll make you sick, it'll make you drunk, you can't stand up, right?

FRANCIS: Even a cranky cop, you say to him, "Who the hell ever gave you the uniform?" There's nothin' shy about me, boy!

dp

Well, it comes from Brazil, most of it does. Some comes from Africa. And people love it.

—John Cipriano

It's available and I take some, but to tell you the truth I'd never miss it if I didn't get it. It's just sort of a habit. I don't fix any for myself in the morning for breakfast. I have milk with my cereal. I could have tea or coffee, I have it available to me. Just once in a blue moon I'll fix up some, but not very often.

But I've never accepted it as being bad for you. They're testing it—I don't know if it's the medical profession or who—but they're testing coffee and many other things, such as fat.

—Neil Henderson

CAMILE PATRICK: Irish coffee is the only coffee you should drink.

SOPHIE TERKEL: Who wants to get fat?

ANN RAPP: Who wants to get drunk?

CAMILE: No comment!

ANN: Who wants to get high?

CAMILE: You don't have to put that much liquor in it, dear.

ANN: It makes you feel warm.

SOPHIE: It's too rich!

ANN STARK: I'm no coffee drinker, I just drink to keep me warm. I don't have to have it. I don't have it for breakfast—some people could die for a cup of coffee, but I don't. I want more coffee than I drink.

CAMILE: I believe in buying the coffee beans and grinding it.

ELMER WALLACH: It's optional.

ANN R.: I think that has changed over the last few years. I buy Taster's Choice and I find I have to use more of it—I'm talking about instant coffee—I have to use a rounder teaspoon.

CAMILE: If you grind it, grind it right before you use it—the aroma, it's just great!

ELMER: I use instant—no waste. One cup at a time, when you live alone especially.

ANN R.: I liked iced coffee, but I don't like to drink it in the wintertime.

SOPHIE: If you put it in the refrigerator you can heat it again later.

ANN S.: I like the Nescafe the best.

SOPHIE: That's not true coffee.

ELMER: They make a lot of coffee in Brazil.

ANN S.: Nescafe is an instant.

SOPHIE: Sure it is, but I always felt it wasn't a true coffee.

ELMER: Why can't they make coffee bags, like tea bags?

CAMILE: Get a patent on it—you'll be a millionaire!

SOPHIE: Elmer, you'll have a Mercedes-Benz!

ANN R.: When I go into a restaurant I always get my coffee right away, and that keeps you going until the meal comes.

CAMILE: Then you have three cups of coffee through the meal.

SOPHIE: And that's not so good.

I wish it wasn't so expensive so we could have it more often. You can have only so much now because it's going up too high. It gets too high.

—Ida Harris

I don't care if I don't drink—I drink coffee, that's good enough.
Jack Mudurian

Get me a cup of coffee before I faint.
Herbie Caldwell

These boys like hot coffee, give 'em hot coffee and they'll be your friend. These guys wait for hot coffee in the morning. *Abe Surgecoff*

What is sleep?

ABE SURGECOFF: If you sleep, you don't have no sound. Unless they get nightmares.

JOHN LOWTHERS: Snow and ice mixed. [*No, sleep.*] Oh, sleep, when you go to bed, that's all, you go into a little slumber.

GEORGE MACWILLIAMS: Goin' off into another world, I guess. I don't know what else to call it.

ROBERT CLEAVES: What is sleep . . . what is it . . . . A cessation of the senses. [*Sounds good.*] Best I can do. It's the best thing I do—sleep . . . . Where's the prize? [*No prize.*] No prize? Dear me, haven't made a nickel in here.

Ernie Brookings: The mind is asleep. I'll check in the dictionary, it could be. Sleep would be an unconscious mind. Would that be it? I'll re-check it in the dictionary. What time will you be in tomorrow?

Well, I like different kinds. I get Sanka. And this week I'm going over to Gable's over in Scotia, they've got a special on Sweet Life coffee under three dollars, there was a coupon in the paper this morning. I've had Maxwell House and Chock Full of Nuts. Chase and Sanborn, I've had that too.

—Stan Abel

Coffee is good and bad, depends on how much you use. Several cups of coffee when somebody has a hangover will wake 'em up. And a cup of coffee when you're on tranquilizers will cut the tranquilizers. Coffee's good to wake you up. Coffee is a good physic to—helps you move your bowels.

Now the bad things about coffee: Too much coffee will keep you awake. That's the only bad thing about it.

—Henry Turner

VILJO LEHTO: You know, coffee is bad too. You know coffee is dope.

DG: You're drinking it now.

VILJO: It's got me a dope, a coffee dope.

CAMILE PATRICK: I love coffee, but I have to drink decaffeinated.

ANN STARK: I can't tell the difference.

CAMILLE: Oh, yes you can.

RUTH LUBRANO: I just got used to it.

I like coffee, but yeccch, that other stuff! I always have coffee for breakfast.

—Mary Grace Murphy

Well, coffee itself is a lot of waste—you've got seeds and you've got to throw 'em away when you're done. I use instant and there's no waste. That's all I can say.

—Elmer Wallach

I'm a medium coffee drinker, about five or six cups a day. (*DG: Decaf?*) Five caffeinated coffees and three decaffeinated coffees—about eight cups a day.

—*Henry Turner*

I will not drink decaffeinated coffee because I need the caffeine.

—*Sybil Robertson*

Coffee in some ways is a symbol for friendship. Friends get together and have a cup of coffee.

—*Ruth Lubrano*

Which do you prefer, coffee or meat?

Coffee, believe it or not! (*Laughs*) I'm not crazy for meat.

—*Mary Monaco*

I'd give up coffee.

—*Tony Villano*

I prefer meat—I mean, I prefer coffee. I like my coffee. I like a little meat, but I still prefer coffee.

—*Ethel Sweet*

I'll take meat.

—*Mildred Makofski*

It's close, but I'd take meat.

—*Sylvia Novotny*

KEN EGLIN: Relax, relaxation. You relax and go off to sleep. Your mind is blank, nothin' on your mind. When I lay in bed, sometimes I used to look up at the ceiling and I'd see things.

BILL NIEMI: Well, it's like large drops of snow that have frozen, isn't it? [*No, sleep.*] Oh, sleep! That's passage of the mind and body moved into rest period to improve the balance of your mind and the coordination of your muscles and your fingers and your toes. You put your body at rest so you'll be able to function better on the next day or on the days to come. It's rest for your heart too.

ABE BERKOVER: You can't define it.

BERNIE REAGAN: . . . [*It's hard to explain.*] Oh, it's not very hard to explain. When you go to bed you lay down, relax and go to sleep . . . . I've got an extra blanket on my bed.

EDGAR MAJORS: You have to sleep if you want to live very long.

LARRY GREEN: Get a good night of rest. Wake up early in the mornin'—five o'clock. Go to work. Shovel coal down at Sprague and Breed's wharf. Eat my breakfast, ham and eggs, coffee, muffins, toast. Take my team out of the yard, Sprague and Breed's Yard. Probably get a carry. You have to carry the baskets and dump 'em in a chute—two tons of coal! They weight eighty-five pounds. You get tired. Probably go on the *Arlington,* the steamer, come from Virginia. It was a soft coal steamer. We'd get twenty-nine bucks a week, and if we worked the steamer we got an extra twenty. A dollar-five an hour. Get home at two o'clock, get your breakfast and go back to work again.

JUSTIN STRASSINKUS: Close eyes.

GENE EDWARDS: Oh, don't even ask me! Sometimes I have a hard time sleepin'!

Last night at dinner, at the cabaret that we had, I left all my meat there, and I had a little bit of that, ah, eggplant, little bit. I don't go for meat unless they're meatballs and, ah, well I like chicken also. Or when I make scalapino. But steak, I never cook it 'cause I don't eat it.

—Mary Monaco

Coffee, I guess. Meat is good. You can go far with coffee.

—Herbie Caldwell

Coffee. It all depends on how much of each you have. It could be a hamburger or it could be a steak.

—John Colton

To drink? Coffee. Meat to eat, coffee to drink.

Ernie Brookings

What a foolish goddamn question that is!

Fergie

None of 'em. Coffee no good, meat no good.

—Viljo Lehto

Meat, I'd rather have a lot of meat than coffee. Coffee's not good for you, anyway.

—Roy Elliot

WALLY BAKER: Meat. I drink one cup of coffee in the mornin' for breakfast. And I have one at lunch, and at night I have a sandwich and a cup of coffee—that's three a day, that's all you need.

DG: How much meat do you have?

WALLY: Oh bologna, hamburger, hot dog, sausage with pancake and a good lot of maple syrup. Anything else you want to know?

DG: Yeah, which do you prefer, coffee or meat?

WALLY: I told you.

DG: It seems like you like them both.

WALLY: Three cups of coffee a day.

DG: How much meat per day?

WALLY: Three times a day.

DG: Same as coffee.

WALLY: Yeah.

Meat, meat over coffee. That's a wholesome food. Coffee—there's nothing to coffee, no nourishment.

—George Vrooman

I would rather give up meat because meat can be tainted. And coffee will keep you awake when you have to drive a car or when you have to finish a job. Coffee is more important than meat. You can get protein from beans. Also coffee is a minor antidote for some poison. Meat isn't, meat can kill you if it's tainted.

—Henry Turner

Oh, naturally meat, there's not much sustenance value to coffee.

Bill Hughes

Meat, it's gotta be meat—what the hell is coffee, just a little liquid. Meat has a lot of you-know-what.

—John Hodorowski

Meat. Meat'll build you up where coffee won't. I have a cup of coffee in the mornin', that's all.

—Fred Delap

GEORGE MACWILLIAMS: I never think about those things. It's just a process of rhythm, same as any animal. They all have to take a rest and have to eat, even a dog. That's the only way I can explain it. A process of livin'—same as any animal.

If you think too much does it make you sleepy or crazy?

JIM THIBEDEAU: Sleepy, I think.

FERGIE: It makes me look like you, sensible.

ED POINDEXTER: Well, it makes you kind of crazy.

ABE SURGECOFF: If you sleep too long it gets you strange, you have to catch it in time.

ERNIE BROOKINGS: It would depend upon the subject. If it was something rough or very erratic it might make you sleepy.

ANDY LEGRICE: Both! (*Laughs*) You're half crazy and half sensible.

FRANK KANSLASKY: Huh?! What do you think it does? I don't sleep that much so I don't know. I'm a very poor sleeper.

FRANCIS MCELROY: It makes you sleepy. (*How?*) Because you're over-thinkin'.

CHARLES SHAY: Neither. (*What does it do?*) Nothin'. It don't give me a headache, that's for sure. Everybody thinks, you know that?

JACK MUDURIAN: Sleepy. (*How come?*) Well, when you think a lot your mind gets drowsy and you think you want to go to sleep and you go to bed and fall asleep, don't you?

LARRY GREEN: (*Laughs*) Jesus Christ! You got me!

dp

Sometimes my little bit of insanity gets the best of me and I have to go take a nap. *Henry Turner*

dp

Oh, I guess it'll have to be coffee. I can't chew meat anymore, I haven't got any teeth.

—Daphne Matthews

Both. Well, I want to tell you something: When you eat meat it goes down into your digestion, the meat goes down with the chewin' and the hot coffee slides all that meat down into your system.

—Abe Surgecoff

That's a hard question. I guess I'd take meat, though.

—Walter McGeorge

I used to like meat, roast beef, years ago. Seems like I've lost my appetite.

—George MacWilliams

FRANK HOOKER: I like both.

ABE SURGECOFF: I'm with you, Mr. Hooker

Coffee royale.

—Harold Farrington

Water! Water! These guys are not used to that water jazz. Honest to God, one time for ten days I was on bread and water in the house of correction. I was fresh. That house of correction was a bitch. It was hell. I asked for it and I got it.

—Ken Eglin

What kind of a question is that? I like steak.

—Peter Kondell

ANTHONY ESPOSITO: Both—I'd rather have both!

DG: What if you had to choose?

ANTHONY: Well, I'd pick the meat.

LEONA QUANT: He asks the funniest questions, doesn't he?

ANTHONY: (*Laughs*)

LEONA: Well it's good for us, it starts us thinking.

ANTHONY: Yeah.

DG: Which would you choose?

LEONA: Meat.

Oh, I don't know, I think coffee, I drink more coffee than meat. I have meat with my meals, but I have coffee in between, quench my thirst.

—*Bernice Moros*

Meet? Who do I want to meet? Gladys Swarthout? She's an opera star, one of the greatest opera stars we ever had. Glady Swartout—Jesus! You don't know her, you don't know no one!

—*Fergie*

Both. I like hot coffee with a meat sandwich. Is that all right?

—*George Stingel*

Give me a coffee and jelly doughnut. I like meat too, naturally. Meat is better than coffee. Give me a steak dinner and a couple beers and a bare-assed broad.

—*Frank Wisnewski*

Is coffee mentioned in the Bible?

LARRY GREEN: No, I don't think so. Milk, milk and honey, that's the lord's supper. Before they killed him, they gave him a big meal. They said to him, "That's the last meal you'll get for the rest of your life."

ABE SURGECOFF: They had some, ah, some, some liquid, some liquid they used to drink, but I don't know what the liquid was.

ERNIE BROOKINGS: To my knowledge, no.

FRANK KANSLASKY: I don't read it, how do I know?

VILJO LEHTO: Yeah, it is at one time. It's dope. If you're drinking coffee you're not religious, you're a dope! It comes off a tree from a bean you know. (*DG: You drink coffee.*) Sometimes I do, not always. I drink instant coffee, decaffeinated. If you drink coffee it affects your heart you know, it's not good for your heart.

WALLY BAKER: Not that I know of. A lot of wine mentioned.

dp

I like to go to bed early to get a lot of sleep and keep the wolf at bay.
Henry Turner

dp

My best drink is water. I like it better than milk or apple juice. Water's good for you any time. Water contains oxygen, which is air. The other goddamn drinks contain mostly gas. You've got to watch out for your health, see?
Arthur Wallace

dp

Which must you have, coffee or cigarettes?

ETHEL SWEEP: I love coffee in the morning, but it was mostly because I'd have my cigarette, but I don't smoke now so it's kind of annoying to have the coffee without the cigarette.

SYLVIA NOVOTNY: When did you quit?

ETHEL: September first.

SYLVIA: So it hasn't been long yet.

ETHEL: They had tubes in me and everything so I thought I'd better quit.

MILDRED MAKOFSKI: She had a heart attack.

SYLVIA: Well, cigarettes and heart attacks go hand in hand.

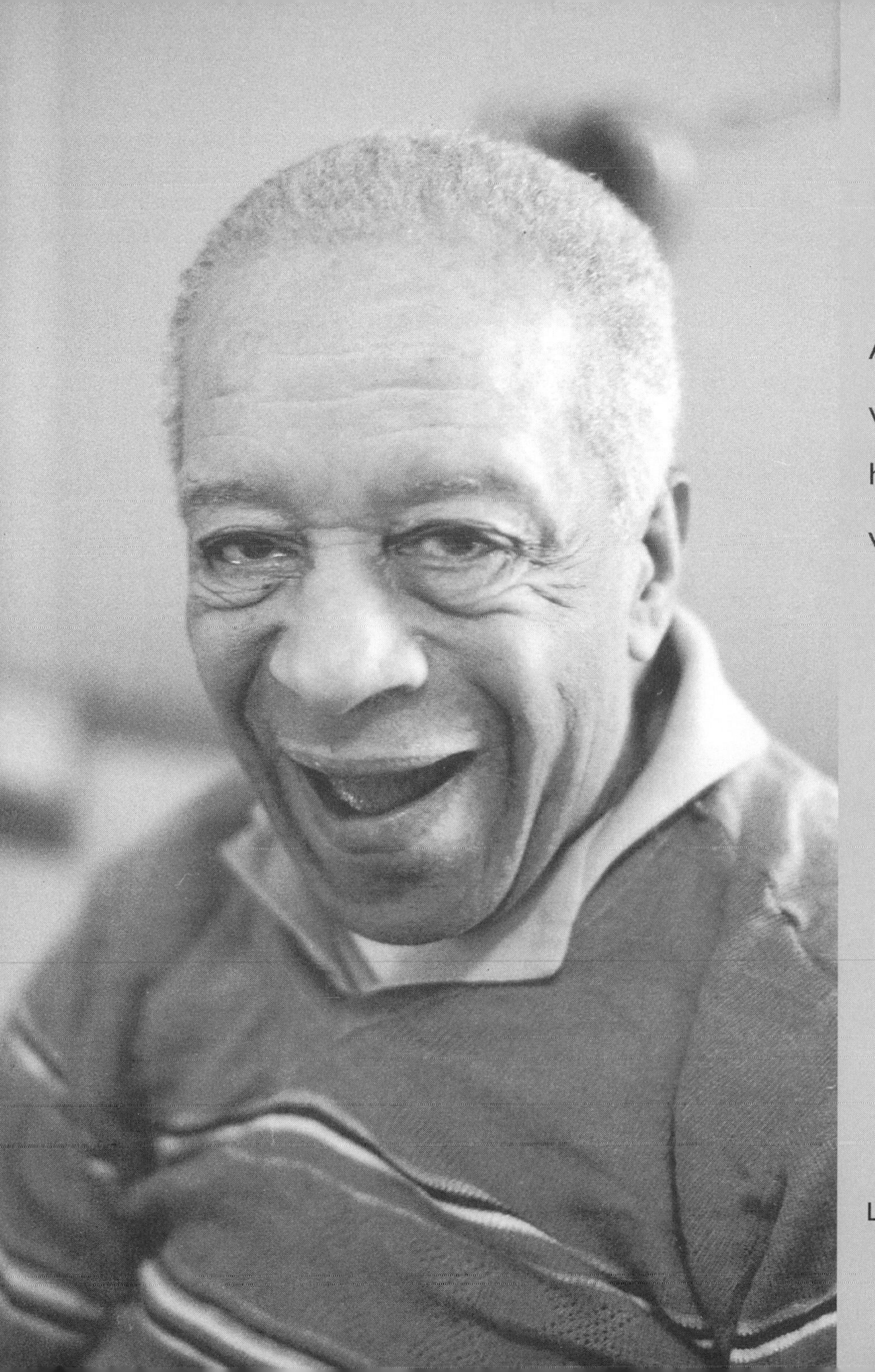

A good blessing will help you. It will sometimes save you from having a physical check-up, which are expensive.

Leo Germino

Larry Green

I got eighty-six hours of sleep since last Friday. Fifty-six hours of sleep is a good amount of sleep for a week and I had thirty extra hours of sleep. And I have another business, I'm starting to sell cigarettes to my friends.
Henry Turner

dp

I heard that there's three different kinds of midgets: biggest, next biggest, and smallest—and they stay small. That's what I heard, I don't know if it's true or not. This guy told me that, that there's three different kinds of midgets. I didn't know that.
John Bitowski

dp

I've got a lot of minor ailments that's botherin' me. Arthritis, mostly. Nobody can do anything about arthritis. It's in the blood. I've got a cold and arthritis and corns ache. A lot of minor ailments. Those things come to all old people over eighty.

Another thing I hate like hell is, on a Sunday, college girls wearin' those goddamn jeans—they look like a goddamn bum. Christ, if you went through Harvard Square in 1908, 1909 dressed like that, a cop would grab you and give you a kick and tell you to go home, don't come to Harvard Square dressed like a bum. Old Joe Parks. Joe Parks was the cop in the square.

—*Arthur Wallace*

You know, I'm all right, Davy, but my kidney's on the bum. I used to drink beer sometimes. See these khaki pants I got on? I've got a topcoat locked way down in the closet. Hope nobody gets ahold of that. I wear that when I go sportin'. I got it down in Jamaica Plain, no foolin'. Geez, they put my cigar out, how the hell am I gonna smoke? No beds made either. What a clown I am. Takin' stuff outa my drawer. What did I take these outa the drawer for? There ain't no beds made—how're you gonna sleep tonight? They're all gonna go sportin' and leave me behind. I don't feel too good. This weather. Barbara'll give me some big cups of coffee and I'll be all right. Jesus Christ, I wish I was like that guy, he's quiet. I oughta get rid of some of this junk. I took it out of my drawer. I got on khaki pants. Oh geez, I don't feel too good. I think it's gonna snow. Every time it's gonna snow my nose gets all blocked up. Oh, I'll be quiet. That brother of mine. How could he sneak off with that radio of mine? I had a brand new radio. Geez, these kidneys, oh these khaki pants. You know what's the matter?—some damn fool put the belt on too tight. I used to work down in the kitchen but I got a broken hip and they're afraid I'll fall. I chew a cigar, but I shouldn't chew it. Chewin's a bad habit. You go some place and you've got to go to the door. No one takes me out. I guess the only one takes me and Ferguson out is the undertaker. No, I won't say that. Ferguson used to dress up. He used to have brand new pants. I have a young niece, I used to learn her how to dance, swim and everything else. I think I'll keep quiet now. I'll keep my mouth shut. I drive everyone out.

—*Herbie Caldwell*

HARRY BRITT: It's tough to get old.

DG: You should be used to it by now.

HARRY: (*Shakes his head*) It came on suddenly, I never expected it.

I'm ninety-six? Well, I can't figure that. I feel all right, I feel first rate. Of course I don't have that bang that I had when I was younger. Once in a while I get steamed up and wish I was goin' somewhere, but I don't let it bother me much. Yes, I feel fine. I have a little touch of head cold once in a while, but nothing serious.

I don't believe there is any advice for living this long. Matter of luck mostly. Ninety-six? Well, Merry Christmas! If that's right I'm damn glad of it because I feel fine. Oh, I have little spells once in a while and I wish I had someplace to go sometimes, but I get so I don't think about it or worry about it. It doesn't bother me any. Sometimes you get a little mad inside, but everyone treats me well—I have no cause to complain.

—*Arthur Brown*

Funny how time marches on . . . but they're all in the same boat here—happy-go-lucky . . . how time marches on. . . . You must realize you're a kid no longer. . . . You're always looking for that first snow storm. What we had the other day—I don't suppose you'd call that a snow storm. . . . About everybody likes to see the old-fashioned Christmas. . . . Nothing like being young. I think from twenty to thirty are the best years . . . but time marches on.

—*Charles Scott*

If I woulda had a brother and he woulda been taller than me I woulda kicked the shit out of my father for bein' short. Ain't you lucky, you're taller than your brother, ain't ya? (*DG: Yes.*) Yeah. Well, maybe he's not too short, so he don't mind it too much. It's not good bein' short, it's terrible. You don't mind bein' average, but short is terrible. You have to look up to everyone your whole life.
Frank Kanslasky

dp

You're not an electrical machine—if you were an electrical machine you wouldn't have to work as hard.
Bill LaGasse

dp

The idea is, when it's too hot, get the hell out of the sun. *Arthur Wallace*

dp

I ought to get a cigar before I faint. You're a good scout. I can't get my shoes on. Will you get me a cigar?
Herbie Caldwell

dp

Hey, Mary! Hurry up! Where's the whiskey? My blood's getting cold.
Arthur Wallace

dp

I'll be fallin' down like a tree.
Herbie Caldwell

dp

DG: Hi, Ed!

ED SHARKEY: Oh, for Christ's sake! I keep telling you, I'm old!

dp

dp

What do you do for a cold?

I'm not a doctor, but Sucrets would help a cold. I wouldn't know exactly, it would depend upon the nature. Cough drops? Depending on the nature of the cold. A cold in the throat would require gargling. One thing I had years ago was Sucrets, S-U-C-R-E-T-S. They're expensive, they come in a small tin can and they're wrapped in a small tin foil about a half inch in diameter. In addition, a doctor, I don't recall his name, recommended Whorehound cough drops. W-H-O-R-E-H-O-U-N-D, I don't think it would be H-O-A-R.

—Ernie Brookings

I'm half Indian. Colds must run back thousands of years. I ask the druggist for cold medicine.

—James Thibedeau

First thing you do is drink Salada tea. The second thing is this: take a drink, whiskey. And, ah, no drafts in the house by the windows. Stay in a rest position in the house. Drink a lot of fluids. See the doctor at least twice a week. And get the medicine and use it—don't leave it on the shelf, drink it. And, ah, the rest period's in bed.

You go down to the drugstore so the drugstore will give you the medicine. And, um, he or she shouldn't get a cold that way, by unbuckling themselves outside.

Doctor prescribes not to go underfed. Oh yeah, and if you have it, have it through the mouth, and the nose goes with it. You breathe in, breathe out. They have to put a towel over their head. I forget what it's called, the steam goes through the mouth and the nose and the towel hangs over the head. And you get all the scum out of your mouth, and it clears up the nostrils too.

—Abe Surgecoff

Now I haven't had a cold for the last three weeks. I let it go and let it sweat. I do a lot of sweatin' and it sweats out. I don't like no pills—I hate to take pills. Now let me tell you the truth of this—I found this out—that you have to take care of yourself. You can't depend on the doctors and nurses, they can only do so much, you've got to take care of yourself. I found this out, bein' in the service: if you don't take care of yourself you can't depend on a doctor, because they're just going to hand you some pills. It's no good. Exercise and keep yourself physically fit. You can beat your own cold by keeping yourself fit.

—*Ken Eglin*

FERGIE: Take care of it. Take some Rem, R-E-M, Rem.

DG: What's Rem?

FERGIE: It's a medicine. It's like manure (*Grins*)

DG: What does it do for you?

FERGIE: Oh, it clears your throat, clears that tickle. And then you don't cough anymore. Just as much, but no more! (*Laughs*) Take some Rem, it immediately takes effect. R-E-M. It's not too expensive. You can make it yourself. You get a crosscut saw and a hammer and a chisel. I'll tell you how to do the job later. I'll write it out for you. And when I write it out for you, you just stick it in your vest pocket. That is, if you have a vest. If you don't have a vest, just stick it in your upper pocket. And later on when you have a cough you just reach in your pocket and take out the Rem and take about a tablespoon full and it slides right down, like going from first to second. You don't have to run too fast from first to second if you hit the ball hard enough—if you hit it out of the park.

Not much to it, it's a simple remedy. You make it yourself. Baseball players don't worry about nothin'—why should they? They can run like a deer. They can run like a goddamn fish in the water.

Keep everybody alive, keep that wheel a-turnin', it's no good to stop. *Andy Legrice*

dp

Sore foot and knocked my shoe over. That's a dirty deal. *Herbie Caldwell*

dp

Tell me if I've stopped. *Hugh Ferguson*

dp

What causes headaches?

BILL LAGASSE: Blood temperature to the head.

ED POINDEXTER: Being worried, toothache—so many things.

BERNIE REAGAN: The wrong glasses.

ED: Smokin' too much.

HARRY KATZ: Too much thinking.

BILL NIEMI: Different kinds of ailments cause headaches.

ERNIE BROOKINGS: Desperation.

LEO GERMINO: There's thirty-two causes of headaches—I read that one time in *Reader's Digest*. I don't know what they are—you'd have to have a physical examination to find out and they'll give you some pills for the headache. I know, I've had 'em. What I was runnin' the elevator in the Hotel Lennox I had a headache one time for three days, I couldn't get rid of it. I went to the doctor in the hotel and he gave me some pills for the headache. They took away the headache all right. It was the elevator, that's what it was, you know, up and down.

ARTHUR WALLACE: The sore throat I've got feels more like a Quincy sore throat than a regular sore throat.

DG: What's a Quincy sore throat?

ARTHUR: At the windpipe it itches like hell.

DG: How did it get the name Quincy sore throat?

ARTHUR: I don't know. Maybe from the Quincy family down in Quincy. Maybe they was the first family to have that particular kind of sore throat. They used to be a prominent family in Quincy. Hundreds of years ago Quincy used to be called Merrimount, but they took the Merrimount off and changed it to Quincy on account of the Quincys owned most of Merrimount. Two of them were presidents.

What do you do to relax when you're tense or upset?

I go down to the cellar and play with my little electric trains. (*DG: What's your set-up?*) The old Lionels and LGB's, I've got a little scenery, not too much, my space is limited down in the cellar.

—*John Cipriano*

To be honest with you, I say, "Dear God, please help me." I don't like to get mad at people and tell them where to get off, I don't like to be that way. I'd rather walk away than fight.

—*Ida Harris*

I just get more nervous! No, sometimes I put the TV on or something. Because when you're all alone you don't get too nervous, because there's no one else to make you nervous.

—Rose Ellis

Through my life I've not gotten excited, because it's the wrong thing to do, you hurt yourself. My experience through life has been friendship back and forth. I spent seven years, five nights a week in fraternal organizations in the Los Angeles harbor area. Learn friendship, see? That's a great thing. From out of your heart banish every unkind thought. Wouldn't it be wonderful today if people thought that way and practiced that way. Why can't we teach each other to be good and honest? People have been good to me all my life and I try to pass it on.

—Neil Henderson

JOHN CATRAMBONE: I'm takin' sleepin' pills every night. If I don't get sleepin' pills I can't sleep.

EARL DAVIS: I like to take a hot shower at night, that relaxes me.

JOHN: I tried that, it didn't work.

EARL: And banana and milk.

JOHN: Banana I have in the morning.

I take a nap.

—Ann Stark

Lay down, spread my legs apart, extend my arms out, close my eyes, throw everything out of my mind and try to find peace with God. That's what I do when I can't sleep, like for the past two weeks.

—George Vrooman

FERGIE: Constant strain of many, many things. It can be worry, it can be many things—too many to mention, we haven't got all day. I am going to leave this hemisphere.

WALTER MCGEORGE: It could be mental or physical. Physically it could be strain, overwork; mentally it could be worry.

JIM THIBEDEAU: Booze.

JOHN FALLON: Your eyesight.

FRANK WISNEWSKI: Worryin', and, ah, if you're hungry it gives you headaches.

ANDY LEGRICE: High blood pressure and rich food.

FRANCIS MCELROY: Thinkin' too hard.

dp

Would you rather have a dizzy spell or stub your toe?

I'd rather stub my toe because you don't come out of a dizzy spell. *Larry Green*

Stub my toe, it would be quick recovery. *Ernie Brookings*

Dizzy spell. (*DG: Why?*) If you stub your toe you hurt your foot and blood may spurt out. *Jack Mudurian*

Probably dizzy spell. It's kind of dangerous, isn't it, to stub your toe? *Bill Niemi*

That's a conundrum! *Gil Greene*

I think I'd rather have a dizzy spell, that doesn't hurt so much. *Daphne Matthews*

Stub my toe. Where do you get these questions from? *George Vrooman*

Stub my toe. (*DG: How come?*) I don't want to have a dizzy spell, I had dizzy spells in New York, due to my diet. I was underweight. *Barbara Katz*

I think of people's faces and stay away from coffee. I listen to my radio and I go to bed early too. There's nothing like sleep to make you feel good the next day. And I also eat good. When I feel tense and nervous in the morning I go to Ruby's and have a good breakfast. The food gives me the energy to think more positive thoughts.

—*Henry Turner*

HERMAN SEFTEL: I like to write, I enjoy doing it. When I'm invited someplace I enjoy writing a thank-you note, which I did recently, several of them.

ANN RAPP: He's a real gentleman.

I like to take my little pillow in the living room and put it on the sofa and I stretch out with the newspaper and try to read. I snooze off and I wake up feelin' a lot better. That's what I've been doing the last couple of days, I haven't been feeling too good.

—*Gert Steinberg*

I lie down on my lounge chair and I relax. Sometimes I turn the radio on for some soft music. I fall asleep and take a good nap.

—*Ann Stark*

Play a lot of those old tunes—"Heart of My Heart"—you know, all those old songs. "I Want a Girl Just Like the Girl That Married Dear Old Dad." That's what my band plays. We play at the nursing homes a lot. Of course, we get paid through the trust fund. Before, we used to donate it. Many times I've donated a twelve, fifteen piece downtown for the polio drive, the heart fund drives. I've got pictures in the paper when they took picturres of the bands. I'm a great one for volunteering music, you know?

—*Tony Villano*

In the spring I go out in my garden. All your cares seem to go—you worry about the weeds! I also read a lot.

—*Kay Cobb*

ETHEL SWEET: Millie told me to take a walk but I don't, I just sit there and get nervous.

MILDRED MAKOFSKI: I have to do something physical—house-clean—pull all the furniture out and clean everything. You tire yourself out and sleep real well that night. And now I've read that doctors recommend exercise for mental patients, so I guess it is good. I used to even move the piano when I had the piano.

ETHEL: If you saw her house you'd see she must get nervous a lot!

I knit, watch TV, and I talk on the phone sometimes. And when I bake I relax.

—*Ann Rapp*

Get drunk! (*Laughs*)

—*Andy Legrice*

Lay down.

—*John Fay*

It's very seldom that I get upset. I don't let anything bother me, I used to, but not anymore.

—*Stan Abel*

LEONA QUANT: Sometimes I listen to the radio.

JOHN CATRAMBONE: Television makes you relax.

EARL DAVIS: Sometimes it makes you sick too.

I never stubbed my toe and I never fainted. That's the truth. And I never been knocked out in any fights I was in, either. *Wally Baker*

Dizzy spell, because I can take something to get rid of it right away. But if you have a stubbed toe you can't walk no place and you're aggravated. How's that for an answer? *John Hodorowski*

EDDIE RUTTER: I don't care to get either one of 'em. They both can be dangerous.

DG: But if you had to choose one?

EDDIE: Oh, I don't know which one I would say.

DG: Then something else instead.

EDDIE: You mean something injurious? Well, with a dizzy spell sometimes if you go and sit down it goes away, so that might be better. If you stub your toe you're liable to wind up in the hospital.

None of 'em, both of 'em are bad. (*DG: What if you had to choose one?*) My toe I s'pose, then I couldn't walk, but if I had a dizzy spell I might bang my head on the concrete. *Viljo Lehto*

dp

If you woke up and were six inches taller, what would be the first thing you'd do?

Help! I'd scream for help! I'd hang off the bed. *Daphne Matthews*

Call for help and wonder why I grew so fast. *Andy Legrice*

Nothing, walk away from it. *Walter Kieran*

Wonder why I had increased in height and wonder why that occurred during the night *Ernie Brookings*

I'd see a psychiatrist. *Jack Mudurian*

I'd get dressed and I'd look for my breakfast. *Francis McElroy*

I'd take a shower and get some decent clothes. *Abe Surgecoff*

Damned if I know! I'd be a giant! *Larry Green*

Get new clothes. *John Fallon*

I just knit and crochet and watch television at the same time.

—Frances Fink

Sex.

—John Catrambone

What do you think about the new artificial heart?

That must be a painful operation to put such a thing in a human being. Generally where the heart is there's very sensitive nerves—it'll probably drive the person crazy.

It's kind of dangerous to operate on people who were near to death, people who might have been out of life's picture, who were at death's door. I don't mean that they passed away or anything, but they have to get the consent of the nearest relative to perform the operation, don't they? If the person is too ill to decide for themselves.

—Bill Niemi

I don't like that. (*DG: Why not?*) I don't think God wants us to fool with our hearts or our insides. He made us the way he wants us to stay—that's what I was taught when I was comin' up, in church.

—Gene Edwards

You can't take the heart out of a dead man or take the heart out of a live man—he would die! If that were possible, someone that lost an arm or a leg, there are no moving parts—it could be grafted on. In other words, it would be easier to graft an arm or a leg, where there are no moving parts. Who are the doctors trying to deceive?

—Gil Greene

Well, he wants to live, that's all I know. And he has to have it changed every six months to a year. They put it in and charge it up—it's already charged and when you bring back the old one it's recharged. They give him liver extract and breathin' tubes and then afterwards they have an excretion.

—Abe Surgecoff

It's somethin' new, yeah, it's somethin' new that they can put in in place of your regular heart. That's something that they've done that's to replace your own. Everyone has a heart.

—Ed Rogers

It's better than no heart at all. It's somethin' essential, you need a heart.

—Harry Katz

That's comin' sooner or later.

—Bill LaGasse

Jesus! It's all right, if you live.

—Larry Green

Revolutionary.

—Walter McGeorge

Well I don't know, you'd probably wonder what happened to you. Your clothes wouldn't fit you or nothin'. That's a lot of inches to grow in one night, six inches. *Bill Niemi*

Well, after I got through lookin' in the mirror I'd show myself off. *Bill LaGasse*

dp

DAVID BREWER: Why do women live longer than men?

FRANCES MCELROY: Because they don't worry.

BERNIE REAGAN: They have an anxiety complex.

FRED MILLER: They drink the right stuff.

BILL LAGASSE: They have a lot of iron.

BILL NIEMI: They probably have better habits about different things, like eating and drinking and washing and taking care of themselves, like personal hygiene.

KEN EGLIN: Well, all I can say is, they dress loose; their clothes are loose. Men's clothes are tight.

Frank Hooker: It's what they don't have to approach in their life.

Andy Legrice: They don't do what we do.

Bernie: Men sometimes do heavy work and they have heart attacks.

Andy: Them heart attacks have only been comin' out in the last couple years.

Bernie: Oh no, they've been having them a long time.

Andy: Yes, but they're, ah, more, more of 'em, more popular.

Well I never heard of that, until you just gave me that knowledge. That's really something. I hadn't known of it until you spoke of it.

—Edgar Major

Eyes are the most important part of your body. If you have poor vision they recommend that you get glasses. And without eyesight you're lost. It's the most important part of your body to have good vision at all times. And without good vision you're lost—it's a great handicap if your vision goes against you. Poor vision is next to blindness.

—Francis McElroy

For all living creatures, the eyes are the basis of sight.

—Ernie Brookings

Eyes are very dangerous to fool around with. And when they get blood-stained, leave it alone or have warm water to soften it. You make more irritation by rubbin' it. The eyes is the most important thing in life. When some of them get in factories they have eye troubles.

—Abe Surgecoff

People have to have eyes to even realize they're livin', don't they? It's a very bad thing to be blind, especially nowadays.

—Bill Niemi

Oh who, who, who made those eyes at me. Who, who, who made those eyes at me. Who, who, who made those eyes at me. . . . That's a song.

—Jack Murdurian

You see good, see pictures, see the paper, see that beautiful flame—that's the dolls, you know. If you didn't have them you wouldn't be livin'.

—Andy Legrice

There's only so much light in your eyes and when you use it up you're gone. Some people are blind, but there's still a light in there. Where do you think the light comes from, your head? That's why you sleep, to save the light. The light you save may save your life. Just like a light bulb—if you run it twenty-four hours a day it'll be gone. There's only so much light in it and it's gone. You've got to be careful. The only thing good about it is you can buy another one. If you don't want to buy it, steal one, that's up to yourself. People steal light bulbs—take it from one socket and put it in another. Sure, it's yours, but it's stealin'—it was meant to be where it was. You've got to buy enough light bulbs.

—Frank Kanslasky

FERGIE: A goatee is alright. I might have had one once, but I didn't notice it. I mean, you don't go carrying a mirror around with you. We all have differences of opinion. How old are you—twenty-four? twenty-five? Well, we don't put any high hats on—we're all getting older. Some of us get older than others. We all, I suppose, put on the dog once in a while. I suppose we don't intend to but we do. Some are younger than others and it's only natural. We're all getting older. Some are good and some are bad and that's normal. Sometimes you don't know who's who. Sometimes we put on the dog. Not intentionally, but sometimes we put it on. Sometimes you don't know. You don't intend to put on the dog, but you put it on just the same.

He was quite a man,

Frankenstein. He was out

of favor, he wasn't a human.

Edgar Major

left to right: Everett Bosworth, George Stingel, Bill Niemi, Larry Green, Abe Berkover, Ernie Brookings

Tell me about cavemen

Cavemen! Jesus Christ! (*Laughs*) Stone Age, clubs, battle axe, long beard, bow and arrows, hatchets, that's all. *Larry Green*

Cavemen were strong. Cavemen didn't shave. Cavemen used bricks to fight the enemy. Cavemen were good fighters. Cavemen didn't talk. Cavemen lived in caves. Cavemen fought together. *Bill LaGasse*

I don't know about cavemen. If it was something else it would be different. I don't know about cavemen. I know cavemen, in my opinion, was this: the cave was shut on one side and open on the other. And they had to live by light. And let's see . . . cavemen were always looking for food so they could live in the cave. The cavemen also wandered through the fields for getting food. Cavemen usually like to have food in their stomach. And also cavemen like to wash themselves up. The go to bed early because they're tired from the fields. They eat and

Who is Frankenstein?

He was a monster, that's what it is, a monster. He was like a mummy. That was Boris Karloff, he was the actor that played that in the movies.

—Ed Rogers

An actor—he was in the horror movies.

—Jim Thibedeau

Why he was that theologian, wasn't he? He was supposed to be. Maybe he never appeared as one, but he went and got the name as actually being Frankenstein, but he wasn't. He wasn't nothin', he wasn't of any importance at all, he was just like all of us—a shifter.

—Fergie

He was a monster. He'd grab everybody in sight.

—John Fay

It's only a movin' picture, nobody should be afraid. If the story was real it'd be different.

—Leo Germino

The monster. He was in a movie, scared people. He's an actor, that's all I know.

—Donald Giracco

A philosopher?

—Abe Berkover

Boris Karloff. It was a monster, he was created by some scientist to be big and strong. In one of those pictures he got burnt. I haven't seen those pictures since I was a little boy. We used to go to the Thompson Square theater in Charlestown and see them.

—George Stingel

Who do you mean, the Frankenstein family, like? That Frankenstein family, they lived over there in Bavaria, wasn't it, West Germany. And he was a doctor, wasn't he? He used to have something wrong—not with him, but with his workers, and he used to ask them to get dead bodies, because they got too cold. They went in the graveyard, these workers, and dug up the bodies. And that was a crime, wasn't it, against the church and government of Germany, so it must have cursed that Frankenstein family in some way that they became monstrous and some of their family members became vampires and they'd fly around. And it was his son that then died, his eldest son, so he operated on him and he found out what he died from and somehow the curse had worked, even though the operation was supposed to save him. And he turned into a monster at different times of the day, so he became cursed, Frankenstein, the eldest son.

Then authors picked up and wrote books about that. And the books became like bestsellers and they were made into movies. And sometimes on Saturday afternoons they even made those Frankenstein and Dracula pictures on television. *Frankenstein, Ghost of Frankenstein, Son of Frankenstein, Daughter of Frankenstein, Dracula, Son of Dracula* and different things like that, et cetera. The old character actors Bela Lugosi and Boris Karloff play in a lot of them movies.

—Bill Niemi

then go to bed. They sleep on blankets. These cavemen also look for animals to kill to eat. Let's see now . . . some live outside the caves because it gets awful hot or cold in the cave. They go back in when it's cold outside. Outside and inside. They make paraffin so they can stay up at night, especially if someone is sick in the family. *Abe Surgecoff*

I'll be a son-of-a-bitch if I've got any angle on that. *Fergie*

They didn't get paid for workin'. *Herbie Caldwell*

Well, they weren't very clean. They didn't shave. They liked to make their own booze out of dandelions and branches. And they're always looking for their women and once they find their women they're gonna keep 'em and kill anyone that comes near 'em. And they liked their sleep—so they'd keep their energy up they'd get a good restful sleep because they always had a hard day ahead of them. *Harold Farrington*

Why, that picture that comes on the television, they lived in caves. That picture on television shows cavemen. He carried a big club and a hatchet. It's on television. He's always afraid someone would take the club from him. The Stone Age. Certain men of the tribe would do the hunting. Then they hang the carcass from a tree and open it up and take all the insides out. They hunted deer and rhinos and elephants. Elephants was valuable for their tusks. I used to sharpen the elephant's nails and paint 'em over, in the zoo. That was a good job. When the job was all done they'd take 'em to the Boston Garden and they'd have that show. One elephant would get up on top of another elephant's back with his forefeet. *Bernie Reagan*

I never studied that at all, cavemen, I never knew much about them. They weren't a bit modern. *John Lowthers*

He's an actor for Metro-Golden-Meyers, the big show business men. He could go from an ugly man to a detective. He was a good actor, he was a long time in show business. Did he die? I don't know, I haven't heard from him in a long time. He was one of the best though, Dave.

—Andy Legrice

He's an outstanding man. I watched him on programs and I think he's an outstanding man and he's liked by several people.

—Francis McElroy

He was a good ball player, he played for the Yankees, he used to play center field with Joe DiMaggio and Keller. And he used to hit the ball two thousand miles.

—Harold Farrington

Jewish, ain't he? I don't know anything about him. I never saw the man, only heard his name mentioned.

—Walter Kieran

I don't know a damn thing about Frankenstein.

Frankenstein was a medical quirk. The doctors injected him with the wrong kind of serum and that caused his abnormality. Once upon a time Frankenstein was a normal human man. He had an automobile accident and the doctors injected him with the wrong kind of serum. That caused him to be abnormal. He walked with a strut. His feet got larger. So did his head. His vision was blurred. And he talked with a slur.

—Walter McGeorge

He's a tall bastard.

—David Brewer

Oh, you mean the one that committed the murder? Wasn't his first name John? Or Joe?

—*Fergie*

He was a man in that play there. He was standin' by the scepter and he was makin' a speech. He ranted and raved, he thought the world was all wrong and he was right.

—*Bernie Reagan*

They said he was some kind of a gorilla that run around loose, robbin' and attackin' people. They finally caught up with him and gunned him out. That was the end of him.

—*John Lowthers*

Well, Frankenstein was a man. He used a mask on his face. This guy had no doubts, and he liked to kill people. He didn't like to live too long in his old age. So the people after a while would dislike him. He himself made a couple masks to kill people for their existence. And well, he was a man that had no fear for people. But when he was in that cage—if you want to call it that—well, they used to feed him, and he sat down and invented medicine. Medicine for disrupting the face and hands. Well, he used to make this medicine so he could disrobe some person, and to disfigure himself.

He said he didn't like to eat any fruit or vegetables in his mouth. Frankenstein also had changed his body features. He wore a suit of clothes like you buy in the store. He was one of these guys that everything he touched people would start runnin' after him. He liked to put people to death.

Well, let's see now, everybody was scared of him and he used to go and smash the contents of medicine, and try and destroy them. He wanted to be in power because anything they would say he would listen carefully.

Christ, cavemen were here long before Christ! I'm sure of it! I read it in books at the Harvard Library and in pictures I've seen. Cavemen was around when they had dinosaurs, those crazy animals.

I saw a picture they made of cavemen and how they lived. Women didn't walk, they dragged 'em by their hair, most of the time. And they killed their wild animals they'd eat with clubs. I'm almost positive, if you look at an ape today, an ape in the zoo, you'll see a caveman. I'm positive apes were made from cavemen, early cavemen. They walk the same. Christ, you can't call an ape a monkey—I can't, no way I can—they don't have no tails. To me, when I look at them and when I see pictures Hollywood makes of them, they look like human beings—like they was human beings one time. I'm almost positive. You look at an ape, really look at it good—look at the way it walks—and concentrate, don't be afraid of it—if it looks at you, just look right back—your eyes will focus and you will see a human being. That's the way I look at it. *Ken Eglin*

They did a lot of writing on the walls, I know that. Pictures of hunting animals on the walls in the Western United States and Europe. I don't know much more about them than that. I'm trying to figure them out.
George McWilliams

Well, they make their own clothes. They kill animals to eat the food from their bodies. They make their own fire to cook the food so they can eat the food. There was no language at that time, the language had to be made. They just grunted and groaned.

Another thing, the cavemen, they don't have a perfectly straight posture when they're standin' up, like you do.
Jack Mudurian

Frankenstein is a figure and he would put on a mask and do the torture. He wanted to be in power and to be in power he would do the things. He rounded up people and killed 'em.

He goes on existing, he starves. Nobody feeds him and he goes on a starvation. He said it's in his power to fix everybody, but he starved to death.

—Abe Surgecoff

He's a big monster, I don't know that much about him. He crashes up everything because he's mad at people—I don't know what for. I don't know what he does now. He lives in Hollywood. He still plays in pictures, mystery pictures. He does all kinds of things, he crashes up everything. There's a Bride of Frankenstein too—that's his mate. She's in a coffin and they experiment and she wakes up and she goes at Frankenstein. He didn't do anything. They, ah, I forget now what they did.

—Bill Sears

He was in a costume, it was his home.

—Fred Freeman

All it was was a story. Some nut figured out to make some money, didn't he? So he figured out to make that thing, didn't he?

—Frank Kanslasky

Was he a technician? I don't know. It wasn't military, no. I don't recall exactly. Was he a magician? I don't recall.

—Ernie Brookings

He was tall, he was strong. That's all I know. I saw the picture—it was good.

—Frank Wisnewski

Frankenstein? Wait a minute—Frankenstein! Isn't that the one that Boris Karloff played? I saw it a couple times. I didn't pay too much attention to it. All I know about Frankenstein is he was a strong man and he stayed in a barn. They had a laboratory set up where he stayed, in his room. He was some kind of a spooky man. He killed people, for no reason I could see—he killed little girls and little boys. He had some kind of a brain operation.

Boris Karloff, he was a whiz makin' that picture. You never heard of Boris Karloff until that picture came. Now he's a wealthy man and he lives someplace in Europe. He's got a funny walk, some kind of an operation he had. That's how they got him to play Frankenstein. The way he walks, they could film around that. They build him up, that's all—bigger head, bigger body.

He's a'scared to death of fire. That's what killed him, fire. The one that played Dracula, him and Frankenstein were in a big fight in one of the pictures I saw and Frankenstein killed Dracula. Everything was on fire, everything caught on fire. That was the end of the picture, anyway.

Boris Karloff will always be a monster—the way he walks, the way he looks. He's the only one they got to play those parts. I think he's retired now. I think he lives in Europe, that's all I know, someplace in Europe. He's very wealthy off. He's very wealthy today, very smart man.

Dracula died, in real life, and Boris Karloff went to the funeral, the wake—whatever you want to call it. And the man's laying there dead and he says, "Now look, why don't you stop playin' dead and get up, you've got work to do—*we've* got work to do!" Boris Karloff made a lot of money on that statement. He had a hell of a lot of nerve to say that. I always said he was a great actor, and he still is in my books.

—Ken Eglin

You mean back in the centuries there? Well, actually they were very healthy men—the ability of 'em and so forth—they was very strong men. What they would do is, they would do different things there and work and make things out of rocks and makes signs there. The health of the men is more powerful than the generation we got today. Actually, in them days your physical condition was more stronger than what you have today and so forth—a lot more stronger than what you have today. See, you take the generation today or from a hundred years and you try and match what we have today to theirs. The old-timers at that time, the strength, the ability of 'em, is actually a lot more stronger than what we have today. *Frank Hooker*

Oh! I never saw one. I'd be afraid, Dave. There's a Mammoth Cave in Virginia. *George Stingel*

Well cavemen, they live in caves, don't they? They have to use a lot of those big stones to make things out of, like to make a table or other furniture. Those caves are kind of cold, so they had to get some kind of animal skins to cover up when they slept. It's cold in those caves. Then they probably ate what was left of the animals after they probably killed them to get their skins. Then they'd have to get some kind of covering for the cave entrance to keep out the cold. *Bill Niemi*

I don't know anything about cavemen. I don't even remember anyone ever speaking of 'em. *Walter Kieran*

They were all prehistoric, that's why I don't know anything about them. They were all prehistoric and I never tried to find out. It's a waste of time. I've got three sisters and they'll tell you, but I can't. They're three glorious sisters. I'll try to help you if I can, but I can't. *Fergie*

Cavemen? They come from the ground. They're big and strong. And they look like apes. *Bill Sears*

He was a monster, killed people. He had a steel bolt running through his neck. It took place in Transylvania. That's all I can think of.

—Gil Greene

Monster. He's ugly, he's not nice to look at. He shows himself to people on the TV set and in the movin' picture houses. And the people want to keep on seein' him more, more, more. He's an entertainer. He entertains the people that want to look at him on the movin' picture house screens and on the TV screens in the people's houses.

—Jack Mudurian

A killer. He makes everybody afraid, afraid to look at him. He makes people a'scared of him. That's his way of remembering people.

—Harry Katz

He's just a character in the movies and on television. Just somethin' somebody dreamed up.

—Charles Turner

I see his picture on TV but I can't describe what he really is.

—Gene Edwards

Monster. Bela Lugosi played Frankenstein. He'd hypnotize you, put you in a trance. He liked women, he'd like your wife. He'd auction them off into white slavery. He gets money and splits the difference with the women. He buys her a castle and then he puts her into white slavery, prostitute. He had her in a trance and she'd do everything he wanted her to do.

Then Prince Charmin' came along, killed Bela Lugosi, took her out of a trance and married her. They lived happily ever after.

—Larry Green

He's a bad fellow, that guy.

—*Everett Bosworth*

Dead people.

—*Justin Strassinkus*

He's scary and he's pretty popular. They married him in the one picture, to a girl just as ugly as he was. And of course he was pretty tall. He'd just scrape his shoes along, that's all he ever did.

—*Bill LaGasse*

DG: What's your favorite monster movie?

BILL NIEMI: Well that was a pretty good, like, monster movie, *King Kong.* Did you see that?

DG: Which one? They did a remake of it.

BILL: They did?

DG: Yeah.

BILL: Well I saw the first that came out. It lasted about three, three and a half hours, the whole picture.

DG: It was good?

BILL: Yeah.

DG: What was the story about?

BILL: Well it was like a mad scientist—I think Boris Karloff played the part of that. Then he's, ah, you know, doin' these experiments, you know, tryin' to make something, to make people change their looks or become something else. Then he found some formula, he could change people into apes—like

What do you know about dinosaurs?

FERGIE: Why, what's the matter with them? There's nothing wrong with them—if you treat them right, they'll treat you right. You treat them wrong, they'll treat you wrong.

DG: How big were dinosaurs?

FERGIE: They're as big as an elephant. They don't bother you unless you bother them, you are in trouble. But if you leave them alone, they'll leave you alone.

DG: Dinosaurs had very small brains.

FERGIE: But they are very effective.

DG: In what way?

FERGIE: If they want to be mean, they can be; if they want to be sweet they can be. It all depends on how you treat them. If you treat them kindly, they'll treat you kindly. But if you give them any trouble, they sure as Christ will give you trouble. You treat a dinosaur with courtesy and they'll treat you with courtesy. We got along with the dinosaurs very well and we treat them very well and they treat us very well. Their lady friends will tell you we treat them very well.

chimpanzees, gorillas. Then he drank it himself and he turned into a gorilla.

DG: A large one.

BILL: Well that's what it was, King Kong—like a big gorilla.

DG: Was he friendly to people or what?

BILL: Well I don't know. He used to go swingin' around everywhere. Then they showed him in the jungle, 'cause I guess those people that live in those countries, like those countries in the Malaysian Peninsula and French Indochina and Philippines and New Guinea and Borneo—people used to be scared when they see that comin'.

You don't get dirty in banks. You go home with neckties on and not one piece of dirt on your clothes.

John Fay

Viljo Lehto

What's the easiest job in the world?

CHARLES SHEA: Detective. I used to do that.

ANDY LEGRICE: Nothin'—if there's nothin' to do you sit down and do nothin'.

BILL NIEMI: Probably like a floorwalker in a department store.

BARBARA KATZ: Having other people do your work for you!

GEORGE VROOMAN: Easiest?

DG: Yes.

GEORGE: The easiest job in the world . . . sleepin'.

DG: That's not a job.

GEORGE: Yeah, it's a job you've got to get done because you've got to get your rest. If you don't get your rest you can't operate.

What was the worst job you ever had?

I could tell you, but it'd take too long. It was a job I had down at the coffee shop. I had to straighten a woman out. I was the waiter, waitin' on tables. She was from the South. She had swear words about Negroes and this and that and I didn't like that. I didn't like it. I don't like people callin' people names. She was a very prejudiced woman. I didn't know at first where she come from and then I found out she came from the South. She was born in Georgia. At first I had to get to know her ways and then I had to straighten her out. I had to tell her right to her face, "Now lookit, I'm half Indian and Negro and Mr. Burns and his wife gave me the keys to the shop to open up and close up and if you don't like it you can hit the streets." I didn't want to swear, but I swore. And she found out I was one of the best pals she had. She found out I was a good friend, a very good friend.

I was only getting $26.50 a week—I had to depend on my tips—oh, my tips were beautiful—it was like workin' in a night club—I had to have a special pocket made in my pants. I had too much change. Change and bills. I used to make thirty-five to forty dollars a week in tips. We used to save our tips till the end of the week and then we'd count 'em up. I'd always have eighty or sixty dollars in my pocket.

—Ken Eglin

I used to kill pigs. It was my first job. That's a hard thing to do, though, you know, Dave? 'Cause every time you see it fall on your face and your arms and everything like that. It was a rotten job. Dirty job. When you go home you have to take a bath and shower to get the odor off.

—John Fay

Chicken farm. Milking the cows with the rubber hose on their tits. And of course watching the chickens. Watching them eat—make sure they get enough. After the cows are milked they go to the field and eat grass all day and then they pull them in at night—they know when to come in. They clean the dishes out for water—clean the hay out. And of course you've got to watch what they pick up—big stones and stuff. And watch the pigs. You put on the rubber glove and reach up in their hind-box and pick out rocks that they eat. They lick rocks and they don't realize it and they suck it in and they don't realize that you've got to pick 'em out. You do the chicknes the same way. And of course the cows, too—you've got to do it to the cows too. They fed the cows pig slop, no, the pigs pig slop. Get it in a bag and mix it with water and they eat it and they get big. And of course you do the horses the same way, and the mules.

The worst time of all is in the summer when you had to cut the hay. In the summer we had to go out and hay. I had to go out and hay, one man. Clean the field up and pitch hay. Put it up in the barn—reserve hay. I had that job thirty-five years. Every summer, pitchin' hay, cuttin' it, loadin' it on the wagon, bringing the wagon in and putting it in the barn and unloading the hay. It was a tiresome job. The place was falling apart, they needed a new barn. I slept in a hay rack. He paid me a thousand a week. The milk went to the table—he didn't sell the milk. It went up to the house and he had four kids—four girls which drank milk. The Mrs. would dress 'em up in the morning after they ate. One of 'em ate nine bowls of milk, I mean oatmeal. They ate in their nighties, see, pajamas. And of course the kids ate four bowls of cereal. And of course they drank eight glasses of milk. Those kids ate a lot—I couldn't see how they'd eat so much. And then they'd come down and she'd dress 'em up and they'd go to school. The old man was sleepin' when she'd change 'em. No one would see 'em get changed except her.

And of course I'm switchin' to the farm again. The mules wouldn't come in and you'd have to get the four of them, one at a time. One walked and three got dragged in. One was a big mule for its size—it looked like a horse, but it was a mule. And

VILJO LEHTO: To eat.

FRED DELAP: Sit down in a chair.

EDDIE RUTTER: That's what I was gonna say.

FRED: (*Laughs*)

LARRY GREEN: Watch people work.

ERNIE BROOKINGS: Home cooking. It's not the easiest, but the most important. Home cooking is a source for meals. It's not the easiest job but the cooks furnish food on which we can survive. (*DG: What would be the easiest job in the world?*) Arts and crafts.

WALTER MCGEORGE: Cuttin' hair.

DG: That's what you did!

WALTER: That's right. It's easy.

DG: Sounds like a good job.

WALTER: (*Nods*)

DG: Why did you get out of it?

WALTER: I didn't have a shop.

GEORGE STINGEL: Well, it would have to be a clerk in a store. It would be nice.

EDDIE RUTTER: Some people like to collect information and run it back to ministers and priests and such as that. That's all I can think of, and I know people do that.

What's the best way to sell something?

The best way—the easiest way—is, "Hey, bub, you got some money? You want to buy this? If you don't, then so long." You don't even have to say goodbye, just go. *John Hodorowski*

of course after they got in, they'd get in their stalls and lie down and laugh all day—ha ha ha. They talked. Mostly everything in there talked. Cows talked too. Sometimes they wouldn't come in and sometimes they would. I don't know why. I guess it was the weather.

Sometimes the cows won't come in—and you have to go out and whistle for 'em—they'd be eating in every direction. But they'd come in if you'd give 'em food. Some of the cows didn't like the gadget for milking because it would hurt their tits. It'd make 'em red and you'd have to put cotton on it. You've got to do that for a cow or else they won't come in next time. It's an old system, but it works. It's fast, faster than a hand jobber. Sometimes you have to bathe the bags because the milk's going sour. Take a rag and clean out the insides of all the milk that's coated on it. They sour in there sometimes if you don't get it all out. The pumps'll take what it can, but sometimes not all of it. And you clean it with a rag and then throw away the rag somewhere out back. It was a nice machine—built around 1940, 1941. But of course you've got to use cotton around the tits, because it hurts 'em. Sucks it right out.

And of course the kids run around and scare the cows. Hit 'em with whips on the can so they won't go to the toilet. Once you rub it with cotton it takes the sting away and they'll be okay. "You okay now, Nellie?" "Yeah, I'm okay, Bossy."

—Bill LaGasse

The worst job, let me see . . . (*whistles*). I was in a position where I had to pick some lousy jobs, some second rate jobs . . . let's see . . . an onion picker up at Bridgewater. That was a lousy job. And picking up stones, fixing up the land so they can plant. That was lousy. I suppose therapeutically they thought it was good for me. I was young. I was full of water and vinegar—I don't cuss, you know what I mean.

And working on the railroad as a gandy dancer was a lousy job. It's a job that the native town men do. They call in men from the town to overhaul the railroad and set up camp for 'em.

But at the time I never looked at them as lousy. I never had a job problem.

I had a lot of good jobs too, you know. Bellhop, medical worker, nurse's assistant. Salesman in my own way, you know, door-to-door.

One part of a job was lousy—when it would rain on the railroad, you'd never get out of it—you're not to get out of the rain until they blow the whistle. You get paid for it, of course. And if the rain'd slow down to what they'd call spittin' they'd still have you working.

—*John Joyce*

I never worked. I was locked up for the rest of my life.

I graduated from high school as a machinist and I did some auto repair work. I used to repair carburetors and fuel pumps. I picked that up in school or somewhere along the line. I worked for Delaney Brothers in Mattapan. I'm pretty sure it was Delaney. I worked there for about a year. I got out of the army when I was twenty and then I worked for Delaney brothers, so I must have been about twenty-two when I went in the state hospital.

I konked out. They got a racket going. See, they've got homes all around the country that are lying dormant and they've got to fill 'em up. You go home at night and go to sleep and you wake up in a state hospital. It's a racket.

In other words, the veterans' hospital or any other hospital is a good place to stay away from if you're a health-minded person. Stay away from hospitals. If you don't like aspirin, take water. They say aspirin relieves pain, but I don't know if it does. Does it?

I was discharged from the place after thirty-two years and I went home and I forgot to take a bath or a shower and my legs developed gangrene. It turned all black and they had to cut it off. It was my fault, but I think it was from the shock treat-

Who invented sitting down?

The man that couldn't stand up. *Bernie Reagan*

I did. It's a good invention. *Larry Green*

Probably the inventor of the first chair. *Bill Niemi*

People. They're tired of standing up so they've got to sit down. *Andy Legrice*

It's natural. *Bill LaGasse*

Damned if I know. *Everett Bosworth*

Secretaries, they've got to sit down and write. Writers, mechanics, lawyers, teachers. *Andy Legrice*

Fred the Caveman. *Bernie Reagan*

Probably the kings and queens when they had to sit down on the throne. *Bill Niemi*

Could it be an Oriental person, in the Orient? *Ernie Brookings*

I don't know. Who invented breathing? That's the same thing. *John Fay*

That's too deep for me.
Ed Andrszweski

An ape. Or a gorilla. *Abe Surgecoff*

Me. *Ken Eglin*

Goliath, the giant. *Fergie*

God. *Francis McElroy*

Sweet Adeline. *Harold Farrington*

Jesus Christ. *Walter McGeorge*

Dr. Christian. *Frank Hooker*

ments they gave me. They jarred my memory and I walked around in a fog and I developed an aversion to showers and baths. It happened once and I lost one leg and then I forget to take a bath a second time and I lost the other leg. I owe it to the shock treatments. I had over forty shock treatments and that's a hell of a lot of shock treatments to give a guy. I still have ringing in my head.

It's a racket. You go to sleep and you wake up in a state hospital. And then years go by and you waste away and you're screwed. And they give you the shock treatment and that's nothing to look forward to. You'd go in and they'd strap you down to a table and put the things on the side of your head and you'd wonder what the hell was going on. I was in agony the whole time I was there. I was always in fear of those shock treatments. And the guy that gave them to you—he wasn't too good-looking himself—he was downright homely. It's a raw deal.

Then they cut it out: no more shock treatments. What a relief that was. They'd already given me forty-two, though. It does something to your brain. Especially if you get a lot of them.

—Peter Kondell

Cabinet making. You have to lift cases; you'd catch your fingers. I broke a case—it slipped off the truck and I got fired. Max Star was the boss and the owner, he fired me. I think that was unfair. He should have just forgot about it. It was an accident. Got paid twelve dollars a week. The Boston Showcase Company was the name of it, at Roxbury Crossing. That's about all.

—Bill Sears

Well, I want to tell you something. I went into the service and they gave me twenty-one dollars a month and I couldn't afford that and I had to take some money from other sources. I couldn't bank it because the rate is small—they wanted fifty or sixty dollars a month. And, ah, we didn't like our chow. They had KP. I almost got into doing it but I didn't have to do it—I excused myself from doing it.

Well, I'll tell you something—I worked in the kitchen, and that paid twenty-one dollars, too. And, ah, I was with the chronical soldiers, chronical persons. Then afterwards they gave me his clothes—it was a fellow that didn't need to put on the clothes. The lieutenant and the major told me you can't wear no booties. Do you know what that is? It's high boots. Then they after a while gave me leggings, legging shoes.

We had to take care of the latrine. And we had to call out the soldiers from their bunks for review. Everybody got juiced up and got punished for it. I wasn't drinking. I drank water and coffee and salad. And tea.

Now, I want to tell you something—we were restricted to the barracks on account of the medicine, they gave me put everybody into quarantine. There was an epidemic of double pneumonia. You had to wait outside the infirmary for them to take care of you when I had a high temperature. This guy, well he went out and got punished for it. He was caught by the MPs and they had a court trial with him. They had to be separated in the barracks during the court trial. It turned out favorable and not favorable because the general, or it could have been a lieutenant, they executed the trial—you have a right to pick a lieutenant or a general. And since they took care of it, it could be called either good behavior or bad behavior. If it's bad behavior you get locked up. And if it's good behavior you're allowed free. It goes on more, but I'll give you some more next time.

—Abe Surgecoff

What's a boomtown?

A town that's full of life. *Jack Mudurian*

A gang of excitable people raisin' hell all the time. *Andy Legrice*

It's on television, Rex Trailer. *Charles Shea*

One that always outdoes it on drinkin'. *Francis McElroy*

It's in-between Scollay Square and Dover Street. *John Fay*

I think it's a lot of people. *Edna Hemion*

It's a busy town, boomtown means they have a little business. It's a western town, that's what it is. *Leo Germino*

It's a certain place, like a village. They have booze and television. *Abe Surgecoff*

Boomtown is a town where they found gold or silver or somethin' like that and it's drawn people. *George Vrooman*

Well, it can be different kinds of boomtown—it can be a baby boomtown or a building boomtown.
Viljo Lehto

It's a place of eternal happiness where the occupants enjoy drinking booze and group dancing. In addition, fireworks and group singing.
Ernie Brookings

dp

I used to play poker at Lamper's Wharf in Lynn. Guys that I worked with at Sprague and Breed's coal wharf. We'd play for five bucks. Put in a buck for the ante. Once in a while I hit a jackpot. Usually went home broke. My wife would be mad at me when I'd come home broke. She'd say, "I'm gonna leave you and go to Connecticut if you don't stop gamblin'." *Larry Green*

I shouldn't have been a damn fool and gone into the army like I did. Look at me now—look at the condition I'm in. I should have stayed home and minded my father and mother. I was a chauffeur—I drove a truck for a chair factory. I had a professional chauffeur's license. One time I stopped by a hydrant and got pinched. I said to myself, "There goes my license." I said I had to speed up to get there. I thought they were doing that just to get me—but they let me go—I kept my license, I speeded up.

—Arthur Labrack

The Depression didn't bother me because I didn't have any money. I was living in Salem, at home with my parents. I worked for the city of Salem for ten years, five days a week. Salem Public Works Department.

I bought a lottery ticket for fifty cents and the number came out 4-1-8-5 and I had it, 4-1-8-5, and I got five hundred dollars cash. That was in June 1922.

I didn't go in the service, I was sick in the hospital, so my brother went in for me. He went in the Army 71st Coast Artillery.

The doctor told me, "You've got one of the best memories I've ever talked with." And it's a good memory for remembering things from a long time ago. I told him about the Salem fire of 1914, and that's forty years ago.

—Walter Kiernan

I help out, I ain't on no payroll. I'm a volunteer. Respectable people.

—Viljo Lehto

dp

What can you get for free?

You askin' me that? I don't know. I had to pay for everything I got.

—*Ken Eglin*

Damn if I know. Everything's different today.

—*John Colton*

Who ever heard of anything you don't have to pay for? You pay for everything you get these days. And if you don't get it, you do without.

—*Fergie*

I don't know of anything you can get for nothin'.

—*John Lowthers*

The sun, the moon and the stars.

—*Fergie*

Free air.

—*Everett Bosworth*

I doubt it.

—*Tom Lavin*

I don't think there's anything around here you can get for free. I can't even get a free cigarette.

—*Arthur LaBrack*

Nothing.

—*Pete Kondell*

How do you repair a toaster?

An electric one? (*DG: Yes.*) It would depend upon the amount of damage. If the heat unit is damaged it would require replacement. *Ernie Brookings*

You got to rewire it. *John Fallon*

Might be a fuse in there and you'd change the fuse. It fits in the bottom there and you just turn it half a turn and it comes out and the fuse is in there. *Bernie Reagan*

Well, you have to take out the burned out part and replace it with a new one. And if it's too badly burned out you proably have to buy a new toaster. (*DG: You make it sound so easy.*) Well, how many times does your toaster burn out, unless it's through fault of your own. *Bill Niemi*

With a pair of pliers. (*DG: That's only the beginning.*) And a nut and a bolt. *Fergie*

You can't repair it—you repair those things? You've got to throw it out and buy a new one—I don't think you can repair it. *Frank Wisnewski*

It depends on what's wrong with it. (*DG: What if there's flames coming out of it?*) Then it's probably burned out. *Ed Poindexter*

FRANK KANSLASKY: I don't even know what a toaster is.

DG: Then how do you repair a clock?

FRANK: Same way you repair the toaster.

DG: How's that?

FRANK: You fix it.

DG: How?

FRANK: Bring the toaster and the clock here and I'm gonna show you how to fix it, all right? I've got to look at it first.

With intellectual ability and mechanically inclined. *Francis McElroy*

Not even a piece of gum.

—John Fay

Geez, I don't know . . . fresh air.

—Larry Green

Can't get no cigars or nothin', can you? Geez, I'm way off. No, you can't get cigars for free. Costs thirty-five cents for five cigars down at Brigham's. Years ago you could get them for a nickel or a dime, ain't that right?

—Herbie Caldwell

I guess the only thing you could say is water, isn't it?

—Bill Niemi

An advertisement.

—Bill LaGasse

Not much of anything.

—Edgar Major

Can't get no coffee for free.

—Herbie Caldweel

Air.

—Harold Farrington

Water, that's all. Ain't that right? Water and air. Everything else you've got to pay for. Just water and air. Walk, too.

—Gene Edwards

Nothin', nothin'. What about cake? I don't care for cake. I like a piece of mince pie once in a while. In the summer I like blueberry pie and in the winter I like mince pie.

—Arthur Wallace

Free? Holy Jesus Christ! You're crazy!

—Bill McGinn

Nothing that I know of.

—Abe Berkover

Fresh air.

—Frank Wisnewski

At Co-operative Bank you can get 1980 almanacs and at Central Congregation you can get a 1980 calendar.

—Ernie Brookings

As far as I know, nothing. You might get advice for free. . . . There's a lot of free advice around, yes sir.

—Mitch Krawzinski

I give up.

—Gil Greene

I don't know. Sometimes you can get somethin' for free but you pay for it in the long run, so it's best to pay for it when you get it.

—Walter McGeorge

Why save money?

Well, prudence dictates it because anything can happen.

—Homer Laviolette

I had a whole mess of bottles and cans. Last summer my friend and I were gonna turn them in so we could get some coffee. We went to this newsroom, Tops' Newsroom, and I handed the guy the bag and he said, "What's this?" And I said, "Bottles and cans."

So he took 'em out of the bag and lined 'em all up on the counter and he starts countin' 'em. The owner of the place comes over and says to him, "What the hell do you think you're doin'?!" He says, "I'm tryin' to figure out how much money she's supposed to get back." So the boss says, "You stupid idiot, we don't even sell soda and beer!" He looks at him and says, "We don't?" And he says, "No we don't and you know it!"

He packed them all back up in the bag and gave 'em back to me and I asked him where I could take 'em and he pointed out the place across the street about a half a block down.

Daphne Matthews

You know what I'm going to do with some of my money? I'm buying a hat—a ski cap. It only costs seven or eight dollars. You can't do much with twenty dollars, so I wanted to get a cap for not more than nine dollars down at Rundey's. I've got a little money saved up. *Henry Turner*

dp

Money you gotta spend or it rot in de pocket. *Sam Vara*

dp

The minute you get a million dollars you're nothin'. You know what you get when you get two million dollars? You get so blue in the face you can't see the cornfield. *Viljo Lehto*

dp

So you can live! Jesus Christ!

—John Bitowski

To pay my bills and get ahead in the world—to accomplish my goal.

—Barbara Katz

For a rainy day—everybody knows that there are days when you can't earn it.

—Joe Ciarciaglino

BOB SHIREY: Because Ben Franklin's one of my heroes and he said a penny saved is a penny earned.

BILL HUGHES: Oh, I hate to puncture your balloon, but what he did was combine much of the wit and wisdom of the world up to that point and put it all in his almanac. He compiled it, but he orginated little if any of it.

BOB: Saving's important because if you don't save you're living on the edge of disaster all the time, and there's no security in that.

To keep from gettin' hungry.

—Andy Legrice

So you have some money for a rainy day.

—Bill Niemi

When you're broke you spend the money that you saved, in a bank or in your own home, in a wall safe or in a floor safe.

—Jack Mudurian

To keep it! (*Laughs*)

—David Brewer

Interest.

—*Larry Green*

To purchase essential items. And I used to save money for memberships in American Standard of Metals and the American Legion and the Saint John's Lodge of Springfield, Vermont. And also the Mineralogical Society of Springfield, Vermont.

—*Ernie Brookings*

GEORGE VROOMAN: To be independent.

BILL HUGHES: Very good answer!

BARBARA KATZ: Yes, good.

DAPHNE MATTHEWS: You're gonna wake up one morning and you're gonna need it.

GEORGE: Emergencies.

I've been wonderin' that, Chrissakes, for years—why!?

—*John Hodorowski*

I can't see any sense in it. What for, for someone else to have a good time on? You kick off and someone else has a good time on it? To hell with that! No, sir!

—*Roy Elliott*

I s'pose a pat answer would be to save for a rainy day. But no, to save money is to have it for when you need or want something. Or just to have it.

—*Bill Hughes*

Well, it's just a handy thing to have when you need it. 'Course you can't take it with you when you leave the world, you know that. It's just a handy thing to have when you're around.

—*Eddie Rutter*

Viljo Lehto Says So, Part Two

I go hold hands with the nurses—what's wrong with that? It's human.

You're a young man, I can pick on you. He's an old man (*points at Wallace Baker*), I can't pick on him, he'll fall down.

You ever hear of a brainwash? Washing people's brains! (*Laughs*) You ever hear of a brainwash? (*How's it work?*) They question you. Keep questioning you and when they found out that you told it wrong or that you lied . . . (*What do they do?*) They can't do much about it except give you a compliment or put you in the hospital. Maybe you're a psychlomaniac or a micromaniac. They put you in the mental hospital.

I'm gonna get me a fly and keep it in my room.

The most important thing of human behavior is don't be terrorizing anybody.

I can speak five languages and I can also blabber.

Then they won't call you a bum.

—Viljo Lehto

Until Getty hit oil he was as normal as you and I. After he hit oil of course you couldn't get near him. I'd rather be me.

—Neil Henderson

You're looking like a million bucks—without the million. How close are you to the million? Forty thousand?

—Fergie

Some people have a one-way mind, they have a mind that just goes forward. And the person with one-way mind, if you talk to them, they don't listen because nothing goes in, only comes out—one-way mind.

Albert Dambrose

Herbie Caldwell

Where do problems come from?

They rise from discussion.

—Abe Surgecoff

Mathematics.

—George Stingel

They come from examples. And now you want to know where examples come from. (*DG: Yes.*) They come from problems.

—Fergie

From difficulties.

—Frances McElroy

From worryin' too much, ain't it, Dave?

—John Fay

Family life. I have a good family life and all that, but problems can come from family life. Work, they can come from work. I like the work, but problems can come up. For instance, I was in cable, that's the installing end of it. In other words, placing the phones in the various homes. Then I wound up in the machine-switching office. The confinement, bein' in the office after working outside, it's not so good being inside after being outside for so many years.

—John Lowthers

You don't expect an answer, do you? That's a damned hard question.

—Walter McGeorge

Subjects of life. Like you have a bill to pay and that's a problem. You've got to pay it and you worry. Worries.

—Andy Legrice

Why do people yell?

Emotional outlet. *Gil Greene*

Because somebody's hurtin' 'em. *Frank Kanslasky*

Because somebody hits 'em in the head with a baseball bat. *Jack Mudurian*

Here's another reason people yell: attention-getting behavior. *Gil Greene*

It depends. Sometimes they might gonna be hurt. And some yell because they've got a bad temper. They yell and get angry at their wife—you don't do that, you're livin' a good married life. *Leo Germino*

To make them happy, exercise their lungs. *Larry Green*

Wherever they start from.

—Frank Wisnewski

Well, there's different kinds of problems. If a fellow, his problems become too much for him, he goes to the counselor and the counselor tells him what to do.

—Bernie Reagan

They're created.

—Abe Berkover

Right here. (*Taps on his head*)

—Robert Cleaves

They just come up. Every day they come up.

—John Fallon

Damned if I know.

—Larry Green

From your head.

—Bill Mctyre

Dead people.

—Justin Strassinkus

Problems come from everywhere. Problems is people's number one headache. Problems is made from other problems, one problem to another. That's all I've got to say.

—Bill LaGasse

Because they're disturbed and also they're unsatsified with what's goin' on. And also if things don't go the way they think they should go they yell. And also people yell when there's really no need of yellin'. It's more or less of a habit. And also, David, an educated person never does any yellin', they take everything that's goin' on in good shape and good manner. *Francis McElroy*

Because they want help. *Bill LaGasse*

To get other people's attention. Or if they're talkin' about something' and they come up to a difference of opinion. *Bill Niemi*

They might feel like screamin', emotionally. Or at a ball game.
George Stingel

There's all kinds of answers, ain't no one answer. Some guy wins a million, he yells. Another guy, you stick a needle up his ass, he yells. It sounds the same, the yell for the million and the yell for the needle, but it's different reasons. *Frank Kanslasky*

To get the things out of your mind. I yell all the time and then it relaxes me afterwards. *John Fay*

To be heard. *Charles Shea*

Scared. And also if there's a fire.
Abe Surgecoff

If they hear somethin' wrong.
Ed Rogers

Because they're suddenly startled.
Ernie Brookings

I'm happy to see you, Dave. You're not big but you're a little bigger than me. I get along with you again.
Jack Mudurian

dp

Where do manners come from?

Manners come from what your parents teach you, from your home bringin' up.

—*Francis McElroy*

From your body.

—*Fergie*

Manners come from the way you act and talk.

—*Walter Kieran*

The rich.

—*Bill LaGasse*

You're born with them according to what your mother and father were or are.

—*Bill Niemi*

Parents.

—*Larry Green*

Gee, I s'pose people make 'em up.

—*Frank Kanslasky*

I would say by acting your age.

—*Ed Rogers*

From people.

—*Abe Surgecoff*

The White House.

—*Harold Farrington*

Why, ah, they teach you manners in the finishing schools.

—Bernie Reagan

Dear Abby.

—Harold Farrington

We learn from one another. If they're no good they get a slap on the wrist.

—Andy Legrice

Manners come from parents. My grandmother taught my mother things too, probably.

—David Brewer

From the sky, don't it?

—Jim Thibedeau

FERGIE: They come from the human body. There are sixteen manners.

DG: Can you name them all?

FERGIE: A, E, I, O, U—that's eight, isn't it?

DG: What about the other eight?

FERGIE: Well, one is in your left hand and one is in your right hand.

From your mother and father, that's where mine come from, please and thank you.

—John Fay

From the mind, manners from the brain.

-Ernie Brookings

Why do people spit?

They have to, I guess, sometimes. They have colds or something and they have to spit it out. *Gene Edwards*

Well, probably because they don't exactly feel well. They have too much mucous in their throat because they have a cold or a headache or something, or they have something caught in their throat. You have to have spit in your mouth so you can chew your food, don't you? *Bill Niemi*

So they can breathe more easier. *Jack Mudurian*

To get something out of their mouth. *John Fallon*

EDDIE RUTTER: That has to be sort of a physical condition.

JOHN HODOROWSKI: To get it out.

ROY ELLIOTT: That's all they can do.

EDDIE: Get it out of your system.

VILJO LEHTO: A cat spits, I seen a cat spittin'.

ROY: I've never seen that, no.

VILJO: Yeah, they do, yeah.

WALLACE BAKER: Nooooo!

VILJO: Yeah, they do.

ROY: I never heard of that, you'll have to look in the book for that.

VILJO: Cats sneeze, too. When cats get mad, they spit.

ROY: They get cat soup too! (*Laughs*) Ketchup! (*Laughs*)

Different reasons. Some have too much mucous in the mouth, some spit because of nerves. Some spit out of disgust, I guess. Some spit at people. *(DG: Why?)* Out of hate.
George Vrooman

They have no manners. *Barbara Katz*

I really don't know why they do it. My father told me once he'd send me right to the middle of next week if he ever caught me doin' it. He said you always keep a Kleenex with you, and if you have to spit, you spit into that. It's very nasty and disgusting. *Daphne Matthews*

Because they have to—they don't like the taste that's in their mouth, so they spit it out. So what else is new?
John Hodorowski

To get rid of a slug now and then.
Wallace Baker

Comes from your iner soul. I don't mean your ass—your inner soul: S-O-U-L.

—Fergie

Well, it's born right in them.

—John Lowthers

Society.

—Fred Freeman

From your mind.

—Harry Katz

When a person behaves himself.

—Rodney Bragg

Human nature.

—John Fallon

What is embarrassment?

Get caught with your pants down. (*DG: Did that ever happen to you?*) Yeah, when I was a kid. I went to a Halloween party and stole my mother's dress. I wore it to the party. She spanked me. It was her new dress. I was six years old. I never done it again.

—Larry Green

JOHN FALLON: That's something happens you don't want to happen.

DG: Did that ever happen to you?

JOHN: M-hmmm.

DG: What happened?

JOHN: Nothing too good . . . I'm looking for a cigar.

Get caught with no clothes on. Or kiss another man's wife. (*DG: Did that ever happen to you?*) Yes! Embarrassing! I never got caught, but I was accused of it.

—*Frank Wisnewski*

JACK MUDURIAN: Cheeky deb.

DG: What?

JACK: Cheeky deb.

DG: What's that mean?

JACK: I don't know. I don't know what embarrassment means. Cheeky deb is Armenian, it mean "I don't know." My mother speaks in Armenian and French and English.

Open the bathroom door and finding your second wife coming in when you're naked. Embarrassment, I don't know; nothing embarrasses me. (*DG: You didn't have a second wife.*) Well, not yet!

—*Robert Cleaves*

JOHN LOWTHERS: It'd be sort of upset over something you've done. Not being on time, you'd be embarrassed.

DG: Did that ever happen to you?

JOHN: Why, ah, half a dozen times to my knowledge.

DG: What's the worst time it happened to you?

John: Around, um, eight o'clock at night.

It's a dirty habit, it's a nasty habit (*DG: Why do people do it?*) Because they got no manners. *John Fay*

To get saliva out of their mouth. I have saliva in my mouth. (*DG: Are you going to spit?*) Not now, when I feel it comin' on with an upset stomach.
Abe Surgecoff

I don't know. Congested lungs. *Larry Green*

There's a lot of causes. (*DG: Like what?*) They keep bringin' up something. *Leo Germino*

They're sick, they can't help themselves. It's a disease. *Andy Legrice*

To expectorate the most saliva.
Ernie Brookings

dp

I told him, "If I had you for a brother-in-law, I'd smother you!" And I'm just the boy that can do it. When I get going—hooooo *boy! Francis McElroy*

dp

Did you ever beat anyone up?

You mean really hit 'em? Yeah, I s'pose I did, I don't remember. That's not even good English, beat up somebody. (*DG: How should I say it?*) Oh, there's better ways, like did you ever accost anybody. Beat up somebody—that's gutter talk. Didn't they teach you English in school? *Frank Kanslasky*

No, no I never did. I would have liked to sometimes. Somebody beat me up. They hit me across the back of the neck about fifty-two times. I was knocked out unconscious almost, almost but not quite. *Leo Germino*

Nope. I abstained. Non-participant, no fights. *Larry Green*

Of course I did, when I got into a fight. You may be the next one! (*Laughs*) *John Fay*

DG: What happened?

JOHN: Well, I fell asleep and I had the door locked and it's pretty hard to wake up sometimes.

DG: What were you supposed to be doing?

JOHN: Reading, reading a book.

ABE SURGECOFF: When you do something and realize that you're not doing it. Another way is this here: well, someone puts something down your back and you can't reach it, so they feel embarrassed.

DG: What would another example be?

ABE: Oh . . . a lady might be dressed in the wrong way, so she feels embarrassed. And, let's see . . . uh . . . embarrassment is you look at the person and the people look on, that's embarrassment. Is that right or wrong?

DG: It could be either, it depends.

ABE: That's right.

Shame. (*DG: Did that ever happen to you?*) I don't recall.

Down and out.

—Fred Miller

When somebody tells you something that you don't like. Or if I told somebody else—that's the same definition. It could be what people say. Two definitions so far.

—David Brewer

Embarrassment . . . well, if you do something right and someone comes along and says you did it wrong, that could be embarrassing because you'd have to start talking in a loud tone to the other person.

—Bill Niemi

Embarrassment is a shock. I got a beauty, and this is the truth —I'm standin' up in Central Square in Cambridge with a good friend of mine and we just got finished drinkin' a bottle of port. Along come these three girls. That middle girl was built! Whooo! She was stacked! (*Laughs*) All right, and me and my big mouth had to say, "Hey, wouldn't I like to take that one in the middle!" And the next thing I know, I was layin' on the ground, rubbin' my jaw. That guy hit me so hard! He didn't knock me out, but I was dizzy. He said, "That's my sister you were talking about." That's it, from then on, every nice-lookin' girl I'd see, I wouldn't say nothin'.

—*Ken Eglin*

WALTER MCGEORGE: Belittlement of one's character.

DG: Have you ever been embarrassed?

WALTER: (*Nods head*)

DG: Care to elaborate?

WALTER: . . . Oh, I've been embarrassed many a time. . . . So easy to think about, but so hard to say. . . .

FERGIE: Embarrassment? Oh, embarrassment means being brought into a case of events that causes you to explain what has happened and how it has happened and what is going to happen in the event of circumstances over which we have no control. It is—wait a minute now—it is . . . very strange that we cannot come right out and be explicit and so alleviate all fears of embarrassment. I don't know, what do you think I should say?

DG: What embarrassment means to you.

FERGIE: Embarrassment to me is circumstances over which we have no control whatsoever. . . . I've got to think now for a while. . . . It is very easy to make a statement of circumstances, but not so easy to explain how these circumstances took effect

A liar is not in perfect condition. Lyin' is only something to make it, make it this way, don't stay in perfect condition. A liar cannot stay in perfect condition.
Abe Surgecoff

dp

BILL CLARK: I'm talking to myself!

FRANK WISNEWSKI: I'm talking to myself too. I'll be goosing flies pretty soon, if this keeps up.

dp

DG: Come on Tom, let's run.

TOM LAVIN: You run and I'll think of it.

dp

FRANCIS MCELROY (*to Fergie*): I can use my dukes and I'm not afraid to. I'll show you who I am!

FERGIE: You're General Shitcake!

dp

There's so many people, it's always quite a thing to keep order. There's always one fellow that wants to do things his way. *Bernie Reagan*

After you get through fixin' a person up, knockin' 'em in the head or whatever, whell, you can't bring 'em back, so it's good to think of that before you do anything. Friendship for all, that's what I say. *Neil Henderson*

I wouldn't hit you, Dave, if my life depended on it. *John Fay*

I'm glad I'm a coward. I wouldn't hurt you for all the teach in China. *Neil Henderson*

Nowadays you have to insist on everything. *Bill Niemi*

and how they were to be taken care of. I don't know what to say, maybe you can help me here.

DG: Have you ever been embarrassed?

FERGIE: I could say I have, but when and where I can't. Many of us have been embarrassed, but when we go to think of where and when we were embarrassed, we can't think of it. When you try to stop and think of these circumstances you're in a smog—which is the same as a fog. How to explain it? I cannot conceive . . . of a relief. What would you say?

DG: I guess you've said it pretty well.

FERGIE: I cannot explain a relief in which we can defend ourselves, and possibly you can. Or can you?

DG: I don't know.

FERGIE: You haven't given it much thought . . . as yet?

DG: No.

FERGIE: Is supper coming up pretty soon?

DG: Yes.

FERGIE: Do you think there is anyone at our supper table who could enlighten us, like any of the ladies? What's your name, Frank?

DG: No, David. My father is Frank.

FERGIE: What can you add to that statement?

DG: I think you covered it.

FERGIE: I'm not a solicitor, you know. . . . That's all I can think of. If you can add a little to it, I wish you would. It is a hard subject to exemplify and if you can help me, I would so appreciate it. . . . I can't think of anything to say. Maybe some of the ladies can. If you would read that off to them and ask them what they think, maybe they could help the cause.

I was never in trouble in my life.

Francis McElroy

Ed Rogers

What's the trouble with kids today?

They're too fuckin' lazy, but leave that one word out. *John Hodorowski*

No discipline. A little whack on the fattest part of their body and they'll go straight. Same with a cow—you give 'em a whack on the ass and they'll go where you want them to go, you don't and they'll go wherever they want to.

Another problem is both parents are working—that's the biggest problem. *Joe Ciarciaglino*

Everytime they do somethin' they wanna get paid for it. *Roy Elliott*

Well, I don't know altogether what to say about that. Some of them are like ordinary people and then some of them get out of the way in their behavior. I don't think kids should be beaten the way they used to, but they've got to be disciplined some. *Eddie Rutter*

What's the worst trouble you were ever in?

Gettin' pinched for stealin' grapes, Phelps' Orchard. I got put on probation for the summer. Gately was the probation officer. They wouldn't let me go to the shows, took my pants off, went to bed with no supper. They said, "Let that be a lesson to you." I was on probation for the rest of the summer. They finally got me off of probation and I got to go to the shows, they gave me ice cream, apple pie. They said, "Let that be a lesson to you—don't steal anything anymore!"

—Larry Green

I was in an automobile accident before, Dave. I'm lucky to be alive. A car run me down; in an intersection I was hit by a car. My legs were hurt and a concussion, too. It was hit and run. It really hurt me.

—George Stingel

None. I wouldn't live to be eighty-seven if I did.

—Walter Kieran

ABE SURGECOFF: (*Laughs*) Can you tell me another one?

DG: What's the best trouble you were ever in?

ABE: (*Laughs*) I can't even think of it right now. Tell me another one.

DG: What if the South had won the Civil War?

ABE: It would be a victory to one of the parties.

It could be the First World War.

I can't recall the date now, but the worst trouble I had was when I was in the hospital and the doctor came in and told me my wife, Merta Elizabeth Munro, died of breast cancer. We were married September 15, 1928, in Burlington, Vermont, on

Colchester Avenue. I don't recall the structure, I think it was a private home. I didn't know she had died until they told me so. It was the veterans' hospital in Bedford.

—Ernie Brookings

Not me.
Stole grapes from our next-door neighbor.
Fell in love, that's trouble.

—Andy Legrice

BILL LAGASSE: Well, I come into town and hooked up with Barb. Broke into a restaurant and took the safe out and ransacked it. Next night broke into a feed store, broke into the safe, ransacked it and walked away.

DG: Still no trouble, though.

BILL: No trouble.

DG: When's the trouble come in?

BILL: These sailors had cars parked down at the railroad—ransacked the cars. The cops picked us up, went to jail, was held overnight. I got in contact with my brother and he made the judge not prosecute. And of course I got off with the skin of my teeth because my brother went to bat for me and I went straight ever since.

In the ice plant. (*DG: What happened?*) I almost didn't get out of there, I almost fell down when I was in there.

—Jack Mudurian

I try not to be mixed up in troubles, see?

—Arthur Wallace

JOHN BITOWSKI: Tramps.

ALICE: Sassy, no bringing up.

JOHN: Well, tramps—no knowledge.

They're brought up without morals or discipline. He who does not chastise his child hates his child. *George Vrooman*

They're getting away with murder. You've got to discipline them when they're small. *Barbara Katz*

Well, they're allowed to do a lot of things that I was never allowed to do—only because no one knows they're doing it! *Daphne Matthews*

Everything! *(Laughs) Bill Hughes*

Everything. (*DG: Like what?*) They get in too much mischief. *John Fallon*

Half of 'em don't wanna work. I ain't jealous of 'em or nothin', but when I was a little boy I had to chase cows on a farm. *Viljo Lehto*

They're too fast, they wanna get everything done too fast, you can't control them. *Andy Legrice*

A lot of kids are out of hand, but I love kids anyways. *John Fay*

They're crazy. *David Brewer*

Spoiled. They want their mother and father to pay for the operation. *Abe Surgecoff*

Some could be too noisy. Too active and noisy—is that true? *Ernie Brookings*

I don't know, they get the wrong ideas. They wanna do what they wanna do. But they get wrong. *Leo Germino*

A lot of them are bad, you know, bad children. There's only a few good ones. *Gene Edwards*

They drink wine and beer. *Pasquale Troiano*

They grow too fast. *Bill LaGasse*

Oh, I don't know, you see an awful lot of fresh kids. *Bill Niemi*

Nothing, I like the kids today. *Jack Mudurian*

FERGIE: I may have been in trouble but not remember it. What are you, an instructor?

DG: No.

FERGIE: You are just you.

DG: Yes. . . . Remember any trouble you were in?

FERGIE: Not offhand. Probably I've been in plenty, but I don't remember it. My memory isn't as good as it used to be. Used-to-be, how long ago is that, huh?

You once told me your age, how old were you then?

DG: I don't remember.

FERGIE: Oh, you have a loss of memory, huh? Is that good to have a loss of memory? It could be and it could not be. It could be good and it could not be good, am I right or wrong?

DG: Right.

FERGIE: (*Sets ashtray on the floor*) Why did I put that on the floor? That is the floor, I hope. It's quite a ways from the ceiling, about twelve feet, I think.

What did you say your name was?

DG: David.

FERGIE: Eisenhower?

DG: Greenberger.

FERGIE: G-R-E-E-N-B-E-R-G-E-R?

DG: Yes.

FERGIE: You mean to tell me that once I was right? Not always, but once. I try. Trying is acceptable, isn't it? Sometimes it is right and sometimes it is wrong.

DG: That's true.

FERGIE: T-R-U-E. What else would you like to know?

DG: What's the worst trouble you were ever in?

FERGIE: You know what the trouble is? Thinking.

DG: Yes.

FERGIE: Y-E-S.

Were you ever in court?

No, I wasn't in court. I haven't got anything to say now. I'm anxious to get my new shoes.

—*Walter Kieran*

Oh, you want me to tell a dirty story? (*DG: Okay.*) No, I couldn't.

—*Tom Lavin*

No, I don't know anything about it, Dave. You'll have to ask some man from the court to help you.

—*George Stingel*

Yeah, once. Salem jail for three months. For drinking. They said I had'a behave or somethin'. My sister said, "You ought to be ashamed of yourself."

—*Herbie Caldwell*

No. It's tough to be in court. I know someone who was in court, for stealing. He got time. Ten years, he got.

—*Bill LaGasse*

Sure—not for anything detrimental to society, I just was in court—not for anything bad.

—*Fergie*

What's right with kids today?

You tell me. *David Brewer*

They don't spit on ya. *Jack Mudurian*

They're normally generally happy, with a few exceptions. *Ernie Brookings*

Their disposition and their obedience. *Francis McElroy*

Kids are getting smarter every day, they're getting smarter and wiser. *Abe Surgecoff*

Well, they're probably more well-mannered and well-behaved and live better than they did in years past. *Bill Niemi*

They're smart. *Larry Green*

They're well-behaved. *John Fallon*

They never forget to eat. *Bill LaGasse*

What's the difference between prison and jail?

When you're in jail you're just all to yourself, but when you're in prison you have more space, you have more space to move around in, after they let you out of your cage, don't they, Dave, Dave Greenberger? You know what they do with prisoners that don't perform? They put them in Folsom Prison, F-O-L-S-O-M. *Jack Mudurian*

Peace. *Andy Legrice*

Great difference. Jail is more, more better, depending in how guilty you are. If you have the sayin' with the judge and court then they find out what's wrong with you and where they're gonna send you.

Prison and jail is two different things. In prison you're locked up for years. In jail you're awaitin' trial. Prison is a serious thing to be in. You don't know who you're livin' with in there that you can trust. *Leo Germino*

Never. I've just sat in and watched cases, but that's all—just watchin'.

—*John Lowthers*

Yeah—I'm the judge. I still go to court. I was the district attorney for quite a while there and a judgeship was offered to me, so I took the judgeship. It's a good job, pays good. I have all the benefits. Two weeks vacation in the summer with pay.

—*Bernie Reagan*

You read about that Specs O'Keefe? He was the stool pigeon of the Brinks robbery. Nineteen fifty was the Brinks job and I got in this mess months later. Nineteen fifty-one I got picked up. Fifty-one and fifty-two I got in bad scrapes. You can always call East Cambridge—they'll give you the details. Anyway, I was down at the house of correction down in East Cambridge, waiting trial, and he was there—Specs O'Keefe. He was in there when I went down there. They put him in there for protection. We got to be very good friends. I liked him. He told me not to worry about my case because I'd beat it. He said, "You'll beat it." They tried to get me on a manslaughter charge. The cops in Cambridge didn't like me. They tried to hang me on a manslaughter charge. They had me down there for nineteen months. Nineteen months I waited trial and I went before the toughest judge in Middlesex County, which is the toughest county in Massachusetts. Daisy Donahue, they called him. He's dead now; he died. Big tall man. Never smiled—deadpan. Another Joe Lewis. Those judges don't say nothin', just sit there writin', listenin' to the lawyers. They threw my case out. They fined me a hundred dollars and sent me home. They fined me for slappin' the girl a month before she died. And I admitted it— I slapped her. But I had to, because of the way she was callin' names, callin' everyone names. That's all they could charge me with was slappin' the girl. The manslaughter charge was wiped out—the couldn't press that. They never found who did it. I have an idea what he looks like, but I never told the police that and I'm not gonna say nothin'.

I never saw that man, Specs O'Keefe, again after I left the courtroom. That last I heard they picked Trigger Burke up. They said he was hired to come here and kill Specs O'Keefe. And he bungled the job and they caught him. They sent him back to New York and hc went to the electric chair. And that is the God's honest truth of a story. I read in the paper about him goin' to the chair.

My mother's in boot hill now, God rest her soul, but she finished payin' off my debt—I paid what I could. I had fifty dollars, but that wasn't enough. The court district attorney said, "That's not enough, you've got to pay it all." I couldn't pay it on time, so I went back to the house of corrections until it was paid and my mother finished payin' it—she paid by the week and I got out after two or three weeks and I went up to Libby's and got a half a pint and went in back of Libby's and all my gang was there and Miss Libby opened the door and I said, "You better bring a fifth of port wine out." And we sat down and I took the half a pint out of my pocket and we started drinking that. And we finished all that off and we got some more.

There was only about eight of us starting off and then we had about thirty-two guys there. Guys and girls. All drinkin' and gettin' shit-faced. All kinds of stuff goin' on back there. You can imagine. We had a guy watchin' for cops. We had a big party. Then I said so long to the gang and said I had to get home and I left 'em and I staggered home.

My mother saw me comin'—she's lookin' out the window. I was staggerin' up the stairs and I saw my cat Tommy—my mother's cat—he took one look at me and went right in the house, right underneath the chair, right next to the stove. And I staggered in and picked up the cat and set him in my lap and sat down on the chair and reached around for the bottle. Then all hell broke loose. My mother got up out of the chair she was

I don't know, they both lock you up. I guess there is a difference, but I don't know what the difference is. *Bill LaGasse*

One you're in for a long time, one you're in for a short time. *John Fallon*

Escape. (*DG: Escape?*) Yeah, out a window. *Walter Kieran*

Some guys say this place, some guys say another place. There's no right answers, you've always got to use the eraser. *Frank Kanslasky*

Time of confinement. *Ernie Brookings*

In jail you can get out and in prison you have a tough time trying to get out. And it also depends upon on your behavior that's in your favor and helps you and helps you to get pardoned. But if you're a wiseguy you'll be held all the longer. And thank God I've never been arrested in my life. *Francis McElroy*

I don't know. No difference. You're done, you're in jail for the rest of your life. *Larry Green*

A prison is really hard to get out of. *John Fay*

Well, probably if a person is arrested and convicted of some crime, and dependin' on what kind of crime it is, if it isn't too severe they probably put them in jail for about thirty days. But if it's longer than that they probably put them in prison. Prison is probably more horrible than jail. *Bill Niemi*

I spanked many a child, but not unless they needed it, and you know when a child needs it. Not when one says, "Go take a shit for yourself." That's not a child, that's a bullshit artist and you give them a spanking. *Fergie*

I was smoking, but I didn't cause the fire on the chair—I'm a very careful smoker. Someone else caused it and I got the blame for it. *Henry Turner*

sittin' in by the window and says, "Son, now you and I are gonna have a talk." And I just said, "Shhhh, now wait a minute, please." I held my hand up and said, "Shhhh, Mom, peace." The old Indian sign, peace. She said, "Damn peace! This is you and me! This is not the Germans and the Italians, this is you and me! This war is just startin'!" Honest to God, if Hollywood was ever there and saw what we were sayin' and the action that was goin' on, they would have made a picture about it. It was comical, I had to laugh.

She just threw it off, though—she'd get all steamed up for a while and I'd go out for a while—out on the avenue with the gang—and when I'd come back she'd be in bed asleep and the next day it would be all fresh. That's the way it was with us.

—*Ken Eglin*

I get buffaloed by the weather. I can't see on the dark days. I can't see to read on the rainy days. My eyes are a little dim on account of my advanced age. But you got to put up with it.

I was in the newspaper business for fifteen years. I was in the paper business in Cambridge when I was a kid for nine years and no one ever bothered me. Then I had a paper business in Roxbury and I got jumped. One guy hit me over the head and I got six or eight bullets in my head. I did all right as a businessman, but that was very troublesome.

A mugger is one who puts a gag down your throat. The Dohertys were muggers. They're all out of business and I'm away from them now. The cops caught some of them. The cops caught quite a few of them.

—*Arthur Wallace*

A watch that's fast, that's ahead, at least it keeps time. But a watch that's behind doesn't keep time, you know that.

Bill Hughes

Walter McGeorge

What's the most important invention of the twentieth century?

BERNIE REAGAN: Manicures

FRED MILLER: There's so many, I forget them all.

BILL LAGASSE: Telephone.

KEN EGLIN: Outer space.

FRANK HOOKER: The latest event—I'd say outer space, myself, with certain judgments.

BERNIE: The faucet is quite an invention. It controls the water supply.

HAROLD FARRINGTON: Atom bomb.

BILL NIEMI: X-ray.

DAVID BREWER: He took it out of my mind, I was gonna say the atom bomb too.

BERNIE: Learnin' foreign languages. There's a place in town where you go there and go to school and they teach you foreign languages.

What can robots do?

Run like hell!

—Ken Eglin

If you bump into one of them you'll think you're on another planet.

—Frank Hooker

They go up to the sky. And they walk and they imitate men.

—Bill Sears

Turn over, I guess.

—Fred Miller

Walk, don't talk.

—Fred Freeman

Change identity.

—John Lowthers

Can he swim?

—Fergie

A robot can make a hole in the ground.

—Abe Surgecoff

I don't know what a robot is—never heard of it before. I don't even know what you mean. I didn't give you no story on the Salem Fire, did I? I don't remember givin you no story on the Salem Fire.

—Walter Kieran

Prescribe things.

—Walter McGeorge

They can't do anything.

—*John Colton*

Oh, I don't know—I got a lot of things on my mind, I don't want to be bothered about those things, robots and all that.

—*Ed Andrszweski*

Why, ah, they can man the defenses. We can put 'em to work. They lift up stuff that's too heavy for a man to lift up. That flashing beacon on their head . . . that's all I can think of. . . . Use 'em to build roads; they can cement as good as anybody else . . . yes, sir.

—*Bernie Reagan*

People make them robots, imitation of people. Like mummies—you can wind 'em up like toys, they're mechanical.

—*Andy Legrice*

Make things. Drugs.

—*Bill McTyre*

There ain't no such thing as a robot. Nobody has invented a robot yet.

—*Gene Edwards*

They're controlled by invisible signals and they obey the signals as instructed by the operator at the control panel.

—*Ernie Brookings*

General work.

—*Frances McElroy*

They'll make their arms and legs. They're machines. A battery would run one. You can control 'em with a button.

—*George Stingel*

LARRY GREEN: Electricity.

ANDY LEGRICE: The space van.

BERNIE: I used to buy *Popular Mechanics.*

ANDY: Oh, that's a good book. A lot of smart professors are in that book.

FRANCIS MCELROY: I'd say peace. And loyalty.

JAMES THIBEDEAU: Space vehicles.

JOHN FALLON: I couldn't tell you what they are.

BERNIE: They land on those planets now and the people are amazed that we have such far-reaching policies.

FRED: They put the guns up on Deer Island.

BERNIE: They had a salvo of guns.

DAVID: What about false fingernails? You know, I've seen people use false fingernails before and you've seen 'em too. I looked at 'em like they were crazy.

BILL NIEMI: How about refrigeration.

BILL LAGASSE: We wouldn't have a lot of things if it wasn't for refrigeration.

ANDY: We'd have a lot of waste of food.

BERNIE: I seen a flat dog yesterday. I seen another one pumpin' him up.

FRANCIS: Kindness.

ANDY: Love. We couldn't get along without it. It gets re-invented everyday.

Can you tell me what a compact disc is?

Who the hell knows?! Write this down: Where do you get all these stupid questions? What's a compact disc?! Where do you think we went to school anyway? That's like asking why doesn't snow fall up instead of down. If you look at it long enough it does fall up. *Frank Kanslasky*

Can it fly? That's something with electricals in it, isn't it? It runs on electricals.

—Ed Rogers

Well, they can live without eating.

—Harold Farrington

I no like them. I go back a Russia.

—Justin Strassinkus

They think and do things just like humans. They can fight. They're good-hearted gents, they're nice to work with. I bought forty-nine robots and now the company's paying twice what it was. My robots eat and sleep.

—Bill LaGasse

They don't do nothin'! (*Laughs*)

—Everett Bosworth

They can do about anything . . . amusement, I think.

—John Fallon

Break.

—Tom Lavin

Anything a human being can do. They can pick and shovel. Just turn the machine on right and they'll pick and shovel.

—Ken Eglin

They can do things that human beings can't do. Like going out in the cold weather that's fifty-five below zero. And what else . . . I can't think of anything else. They can't eat, people can eat. They can't smoke. They can't wear clothes and hats. You've got to oil them, put gas and oil in them.

—Jack Mudurian

Just about anything, I guess.

—*Jim Thibedeau*

Shoots up in the air and explodes up in the air.

—*Abe Surgecoff*

Sears and Robots you mean? (*Laughs*)

—*John Fay*

Oh, mechanical men. They walk around, they set the table and don't say nothin'. They bring you your underwear and they put you to bed. They take out a cigar and smoke cigars. They stand there and watch you. Mechanical men. Christ, they wash windows, shovel snow, give you a cigar, put out the lights. And they wave good night.

—*Larry Green*

If my robot works, there's an outlet down at the Greyhound bus terminal and I'll demonstrate it and you bring a movie camera and take pictures of it. I'll have the robot done by the middle of March or the middle of April.

—*Henry Turner*

What's a word processor?

He makes words out of other words. Like did can say did backwards, D-I-D. *Harold Farrington*

A person who understands and knows so many words and so much English. *Bernie Reagan*

Processor? Producer—producin' the progress, progress ahead. Progressin'. *Andy Legrice*

It's some kind of a new machine, isn't it, that was invented to put words in their correct place, so people can understand them properly. Sometimes it's hard to read printing. *Bill Niemi*

I never heard of that word, so I can't help you out. I thought you said "prostitute" at first. I don't know what that word means, though. I'd like to help you out, but I'm not college material like Johnny Fay! I know a little, but not a lot. *Frank Wisnewski*

I don't know. I don't know if it's somethin' to drink or eat or what. *John Fay*

Profound, they're profound. *Harry Katz*

To process words, to break it down. To process a man is to get rid of him from the service, to let him go—it's a discharge from the services—army, navy, Coast Guard. *George Stingel*

A word processor would be to arrange words to express past events and thought, is that true? It could be verbally or written. *Ernie Brookings*

Somebody that discusses words, on a subject, like a debate. *Ed Rogers*

A guy that works at the city hall and watches out for the work to be done. He attends to processes around the office. The processor is like a judge, but don't write that down. *Abe Surgecoff*

It's one that gains, a prospector. *Francis McElroy*

That means somebody that done something. *Walter Kieran*

One that measures gold. He doesn't make it, it's already made—he finds it. It isn't glued together or anything, it's just gold, G-O-L-D. *Fergie*

Somebody that figures out things. He figures out the cost of everything, he's a processor. *John Fallon*

If you had a robot what would you want it to do for you?

LEONA QUANT: Could I be riding it? Is it a robot to ride? That's what I'd want to do.

EARL DAVIS: I s'pose I could have it clean my house for me, 'cause I'm too lazy to do housework. After my mother died my father said, "I'm going to do a minimum amount of dusting because your mother went crazy chasing every bit of dust." My father was on the road a lot for GE and my mother was an artist.

ANDY LEGRICE: Drink beer with ya.

JOHN FAY: Talk back.

ANDY: Sleep over! (*Laughs*) Got to work, pick and shovel. Dig a ditch so I could stick it in a ditch! (*Laughs*)

JOHN CATRAMBONE: Stop the war.

ED ROGERS: Oh, if I had a robot I'd want it to perform.

DG: What's the difference between addition and multiplication?

TOM LAVIN: Three letters.

DG: What's the difference between addition and subtraction?

JOHN COLTON: One's going in and the other's coming out.

DG: How do you find the square root of a number?

LARRY GREEN: A bottle of tonic.

DG: What is mathematics?

FERGIE: Mathematics is addition. I can also be multiplication or division or subtraction.

DG: How important is arithmetic?

HERBIE CALDWELL: Oh, it's pretty important.

FERGIE: It's on of the most important words in the dictionary. So is multiplication. And so is subtraction.

LARRY: Very important. It's the first thing you learn when you go to school.

TOM: It isn't.

FERGIE: It's very important.

HERBIE: It's important, all right.

JOHN: Very important. You add, subtract and multiply. There's more to it than that . . . geometry and so forth. Multiplication . . . addition . . . subtraction . . . mathematics—that's the name for it.

How can you tell if someone's a genius?

If they prove themselves to show something they did to show they're a genius.

—Dora Gurkewitz

They excel in something.

—Anne Rapp

By watching what they're doing and comparing them to another person.

—Ann Stark

I never even heard of it before, so how can I tell you what it is? You're not gonna write *that* down, are you? *Gene Edwards*

Obviously I don't know at the present. Is everything all right? Can I have a cigarette? *Ed Poindexter*

I hear my aunt's voice and my mother's voice night and day. I lay down and try to sleep and I hear their voices. I don't know if it's a recording or some modern gadget or what. *Richard Smith*

I'm living in a timeless world now. During the night all my electronic watches pooped out, all around the same time, around two-thirty. The batteries had all run their life out, about two years. I thought it was a strange coincidence to have four watches all poop out at the same time like that, of course I bought them all at the same time. *Bill Hughes*

Radio is a marvelous invention. It brought mankind out of the wee hours and put him right back up where he belongs. *Walter McGeorge*

By the remarkable things they do.

—Ruth Lubrano

I don't think it's always noticeable on somebody.

—Sybil Robertson

You gotta be smart to be able to tell.

—David Brewer

Well, if they know something special about different people or different ideas or different lands or whatever they have—planets and things like that. People can live on these extra planets that are supposed to be up in the heavens.

—Bill Niemi

GERT STEINBERG: Well, I had a friend who's a genius and I'd like to see her help others.

ANNE RAPP: She doesn't have a friend who's a genius.

GERT: No, I don't have a friend who's a genius, I said if I did.

By the way they talk. You know—when you're talking and the things you say. Okay? I have a grandson and he's a genius. The way he says things—my Daddy fixed this, my Daddy fixed that—but he's two steps ahead of his daddy too.

—Mary Pieszczoch

I'd say sometimes it's the self-made man that becomes a genius—it isn't education, it's what you are.

—Ann Law

I think a genius is born and they excel, but it can be in just one thing, it doesn't have to be in everything to be a genius.

—Anne Rapp

By their knowledge, and the way they speak and what they're doing. And if it's a child who's a genius you can tell by their actions.

—*Ann Stark*

You can't. There's a fine line between genius and other people.

—*Homer Law*

What can you tell me about gravity?

That Theodore Newton one hot sunny summer afternoon in the seacoast town in southern France on the Mediterranean coast where he had some kind of farm—he was a scientist or a chemist—and he had an apple orchard too, and he was sitting under an apple tree with a pen or pencil and a pad of paper and he was figuring out the law of gravity, and the he discovered the right theory and he was so happy he yelled out, "Eureka, I've discovered it!" Then he was gonna get up, you know, from his sittin' position and an apple fell right on his head. That probably proved to him double that the law of gravity works. What's the sense of provin' something if it doesn't work? Probably made him feel good.

That's in a history book, too. It's a required subject.

—*Bill Niemi*

Gravity—I've heard the word, but I've never cased it. Give me a hint—what is gravity? (*DG: It's what keeps you from floating off into space.*) Oh. Yeah. Well, I believe in gravity. And I believe in planets, I do believe in planets—they're up there, floatin' around. And they know everything that's going on here. They got these countries based, cased, hooked and booked.

Mr. Bell started the phone company with a couple of wires and two receivers. Then it was built up into a machine-switching arrangement over a matter of years. That's when I took control of it—made myself into a multi-millionaire. I put the money on the line to build it up. They call it the Bell Telephone. They have a sign of a bell—they draw a picture of a bell there. You've seen them signs plenty. Some of these fellas that fix up and arrange signs designed it. To begin with, I paid for it. And then after that those usin' the phones paid for it, when we started to add to it and build it up. [*Do you get free use of the telephone?*] No, to tell you the truth I don't—I've been payin' right along and I own the company. I could have had free use if I'd've gone after it, but I didn't. *John Lowthers*

dp

There's two words I don't know how to spell: job and work. Run—I know how to spell that. And the cops know that. *Ken Eglin*

Money's only the bread of life. If you ain't got no money you ain't got no bread of life. And if you ain't got money you ain't human. Only humans take money. They say are you a dog or a cat or a raccoon or elephant? That's how they look at it—I'm only explaining, I'm not trying to make no hard feelings between humans. *Viljo Lehto*

I am not going by Hollywood, no, I'm goin' by my thoughts, my sights, my seein'. My mind is tellin' me this, my brain. The planets, one day they're gonna land on this planet, and they're gonna scare the hell out of this world. They're not gonna scare me, though. There's not a damn thing in the world that scares me. I don't know how I got that way.

—*Ken Eglin*

Gravity is oxygen that it takes and eliminates the air and you can't breathe. Gravity also, you can't live without gravity, you have to have gravity. Gravity is another thing that you cannot get around, gravity is not to move around, your oxygen is worn out. And another thing, you can't hold anything in your hand or the gravity would be forced to take it away and you're a dead guy if property comes down, down on the ground.

—*Abe Surgecoff*

We're better than machines, we can reproduce ourselves, through sex—a machine can't. I'm looking for a young girl under forty to marry me. We're better than the best robot and we're better than the best computer, we are. Another thing we can do that a robot can't is climb a ladder and paint the side of a house.

—*Henry Turner*

You can't pull the eyes over mama, mama knows everything. That's what they're here for.

Ken Eglin

Francis McElroy

What's the most important thing to teach a child?

Intelligence. And make sure that the child doesn't wander away from home and get lost. *Ernie Brookings*

Obedience, good duty, kindness, faithfulness—that's all I know for now. *Andy Legrice*

Behave itself, 'cause when it gets older it's got to know something. *David Brewer*

Not to eat with his hands. *Frank Kanslasky*

To love his mother. *Abe Berkover*

Cleanliness and godliness. *George Stingel*

Good manners. *Bill LaGasse*

My mother was a good woman, a hard worker. Good at washin' and everything else. Good at clothes-hangin'. Once in a while she'd sing. And the kids could join in too. She ran the house. We all worked and helped to pay rent. Sometimes she'd wear a gingham dress or something. My mother's been dead a long time.

—Herbie Caldwell

I had a very good mother. Kept me out of trouble. For me, that was hard to do. There were twelve kids—six boys, six girls. John, Joe, Andy, Louis, Billy and me. Virginia, Frances, Mildred, Statia, Margaret and Jane. I was number eight. She brought us all into the world and she kept us busy pretty well.

—Frank Hooker

When I was little she nursed me. She used to iron my clothes and make my lunch to go to school. She'd take me out to the Olympia to the show. We used to go to Revere.

When I was bad she used to put me to bed early with no supper. I was six years old. She was a good cook. Apple pies, veal cutlets, chicken, beef stew, chocolate eclairs, strawberry shortcake, a glass of milk. When I was older I used to go to a beer joint—Pete's Beer Joint. Six glasses of ale for a quarter.

—Larry Green

My mother, well she was a quiet, loving, well-spoken person. She was sick for a long time, had probably some kind of heart trouble. And she liked to work in the family flower garden. And, ah, she came from the old country, from the western section of Finland. And she all of a sudden decided one day to come to America! (*Laughs*)

She loved in her own way to cook the meals and everything. She didn't like to be disturbed when she was cookin'. I used to cook when she was sick and my father was sick for a while there too—he'd get awful headaches, especially after dinner on

Sundays. They like to go visit when they were feelin' all right. And she loved the spaghetti I used to cook. I'd cook her a plate of spaghetti on Friday nights.

—Bill Niemi

My memory's poor. I was thankful to have a mother.

—John Colton

My mother is 166 years old, has tits and two legs and two arms and a good set of teeth. She weighs 166 pounds—that's a lot of weight for a woman; 168; 170. Sometimes she gets up to 200, when she eats a little bit too much. She's kind, very kind and very graceful. Very pretty. She's not like I am, homely—she's a pretty girl. (*DG: How does she live so long?*) Well, she eats everything I eat—potatoes, roast beef, roast cabbage, peas, string beans, carrots. She drinks plenty of water—about a quart a day. A quart to two quarts. Four quarts to a gallon. She drinks a gallon every day. A gallon isn't too much. Enough to drown, but it's only enough to drink. You could drink a gallon and not think a thing about it. We're made up of water. Exactly eight gallons. You didn't know that, did you? Eight gallons of water to a human being.

—Fergie

Well, she's, ah—we had a store and we used to work in the store—Reagan's Cigar Store in East Boston. We had a roomin' house and she ran the roomin' house. We made it into flats afterwards—apartments, kitchenette apartments.

She used to go to church and come home and take care of the house. She had a book right there with the registration of the people in the house—the tenants. The law compels you to keep a record of people who live in your house.

—Bernie Reagan

Oh, ah, well, the most important thing to teach a child is to, ah, you know, to obey somethin'—his mother, whatever his mother tells him to do. *Ed Rogers*

Manners, good manners—please, thank you, I love you. *Larry Green*

Feed 'em. *Pasquale Troiano*

To go to the toilet. *Charles Shea*

Manners. I wanna tell you something: they have to learn when to make the duty and when not to make the duty, that's manners. *Abe Surgecoff*

Keep after 'em and make 'em do what's best, or promise 'em you won't do anything for 'em unless they do what you want 'em to. *Leo Germino*

Probably to respect other people's feelings, 'cause a lot of times people say things, you know, and really hurt you. *Bill Niemi*

Well, offhand I can't think of anything, Dave. *Jack Mudurian*

dp

I like beer, but I don't love it. Some people put their face in it, but I don't. I like a glass of beer like any boy. Any man, woman or child. I like beer, but I don't love it.

One thing I do love is children. I adore them. Children are the makers of our land. What those children do later on we've done already, but they're gonna do it over. And if we show them a good example, they'll show us a good example. If we show them the right way they'll follow that lead. And if we show them a dirty rotten trick they'll follow that trick. If we show them the right road, they'll take that right road, but if we show them the wrong road, they'll take that dirty wrong road.

A lot of children will take their father's advice and their mother's advice and they'll pool it, and see which comes out best. You know, children aren't so dumb as you think. They'll say, "Let's just team them up and see which one wins." And invariably the mother will win. Children will argue. One will say, "Don't you think Mother's right?" and the other will say, "Yes, but we've got to give Father a break." *Fergie*

dp

She passed away. Deceased. She was very good to me, I always got along good with my parents. She lived quite a few years. She was healthy and happy. And she was the mother of five children—three boys and two girls. And she always kept a good home for us. She got along with everybody.

—Frances McElroy

My mother was a very likable person. My mother raised a dump. That's a dump that's a hole in the earth and she had to fill it up with ashes. She worked on the land there, for hours. She builded a garage, a five-car garage and, ah, she liked the yard.

She was a religious person. One time she asked my father to help her out and my father said, "You should, ah, take it easy," but she couldn't take it easy. Ah, well, she bought a home on a dump and, ah . . . wait a minute . . . oh, yeah—she made ends meet.

Next thing is that she used to make dresses. She made a dress for my sister and everybody admired it in the street.

And she loved the fruit of the trees. She planted many trees. Let's see, apple trees she had, plum trees and a vegetable garden—a big large vegetable garden on the land.

And, let's see now, she used to do her own paintin', in the home. She just knows how to do it, see.

She loved a car. She wanted to buy a car and she saved enough money to buy the car.

She was loved by my father very much.

Let's see now—oh, yeah—the garages there had a cellar underneath and she helped the contractors how to build it.

And everybody liked her for her generous ways, like the Bible, in generous. She helped the neighborhood too.

My mother sat up late hours to do the cloth material, patches and housework. She made ends meet, she had a room with all her personal property and didn't have to borrow anyone else's things. That's how she was.

—Abe Surgecoff

When my mother passed away they got me out of the army. The lieutenant knew my mother from dancin' all the time. I guess she got sick and that was it. I forget the name of the church . . . St. Mary Cecile's in Charlestown. It was like Capen Hall—dancin', jitter-buggin'—that was how I learned to dance before my mother passed away. She used to dance with one of the big shots—what would you call it? . . . Oh, right on the tip of my tongue. . . . I can't think of it.

Before my mother passed away she said, "Ill teach you how to dance," which she did, she taught me how to dance.

—*John Fay*

My mother's 200 years old. She's about six-foot-two. I don't know no more to tell you.

—*Bill LaGasse*

Well, I'll say she was the best. A 100-percent mother. Did everything a mother possibly could do, without any complaints. And when she did get mad at us she'd have a really good whack. She had all boys and she could really keep us under control. And she could cook a really good meal. She's in a nursing home now and she's 84.

—*Harold Farrington*

She won 500 bucks one time, gambling. She brought up a big family. I think about four sisters and five brothers. They all had good jobs.

—*Fred Miller*

She used to like to trim hats and she was forever dressing the children up. That's about all I can remember about her, that's a long time ago.

—*John Lowthers*

My father loved blues music and he'd come home at two in the morning and wake me up and say, "Ruthie, here's a turkey sandwich,"—with Russian dressing, that was our favorite—"but don't tell your brothers and sisters. Shhhhh!" And I believed him. But what he was doing was going down the hall to the other's rooms and saying the same thing to them and giving each one of them a sandwich.

He made us all feel special, that's what that was all about. Then when he was all done he'd say, "Ruthie, sing 'Saint James Infirmary' for me." He'd sit in his rocker—it was actually what they called a Morris chair, and his name was Morris. I'd say, "What do you want me to sing?" And he'd say, "You know," and I'd sing 'Saint James Infirmary.' (*Sings part of the song, with Sybil Robertson joining in and the two of them punctuating their exuberant singing with hand claps*) He'd sit there and smile and my mother would get mad at him for waking all the kids up so late. She'd say, "Look at him sitting there with his nostrils all extended, he's all excited!" *Ruth Lubrano*

dp

DG: Charlie, what kind of work did you do?

CHARLIE JOHANSON: I was a kid. My mother gave me money. And my father took it away.

She's in boot hill now. I buried my mother in '71—November the 20th, 1971. I told her, "You stay home. I don't want you to work. I don't want you to even spell that word. You take it easy, I'll pay the rent and the phone bill." And I meant every word I said, I swear it. And she knew I meant what I said because she saw the tears comin' from my eyes.

—*Ken Eglin*

I feel like an answer goin'
around waitin' for the proper
question this morning.

Bob Shirey

Charlie Hewis

Tell me something important to write down.

To love, honor and obey everyone, and to help everyone. *Francis McElroy*

Stay home. *Andy Legrice*

Always mind your manners and help those who are less fortunate. *Bill Niemi*

Make friends with everybody. *Andy Legrice*

Why, ah, I'd say the next meal, I guess. *John Lowthers*

Chop suey sandwiches. *Fergie*

The weather, changeable every time. *John Fay*

About the individual, how he gets along. *Abe Surgecoff*

The movin' picture we took the other day over in the room there, that was important. *Bill Sears*

Did the future turn out the way you thought it would?

Did the future turn out the way I thought it would? Well, no. That's a question! Did the future turn out the way you thought it would? No. I never thought it would turn out the way it is now, I would say no. Before, it was different. I mean a lot of things were different before than they are now. It's changed now, it's a lot—it's altogether different now. (*DG: Do you like how it turned out?*) Well, it's okay. I don't think it's any different than it was before, than it was before. So it's all the same, I mean, I think it's all the same.

—Ed Rogers

No—does it ever? I don't think it does for anybody. I'm appalled by the way it turned out! (*Laughs*) But, it could've been worse, could've been a lot worse.

—Bob Shirey

I never thought about nothing like that, no, no. I was a common slave, workin'. Common slave. You know when you're drinkin' Budweiser you're only a slave. That's fifty years ago.

What about the ox—I drove ox when I was nine years old. What about the chestnut trees—the blight came along and killed 'em off. We used to have a lot of chestnut trees. We were young and jumpin' around and everything disappeared, up and died. Blight killed the trees.

—Viljo Lehto

FRANCIS MCELROY: No, and to tell you the God's honest truth, Dave, it's gettin' worse instead of better. Am I right, Walter?

WALTER KIERAN: Yes.

FRANCIS: Walter says I'm right!

No, I wish it would. But why worry about it—if the future didn't turn out that way, it may yet. Life is a good thing and you mustn't let anything discourage you, you have to get along.
—*Leo Germino*

Yes, sure, it's the way the people live.
—*Walter Kieran*

Oh yeah, it's good! Things are gettin' better all the time!
—*Andy Legrice*

WALTER MCGEORGE: No.

DG: How so?

WALTER: I thought I'd be a rich man.

DG: Doing what?

WALTER: Barbering.

Does everything belong to someone?

JOHN LOWTHERS: Why, practically.

DG: What do you mean?

JOHN: Well most of it.

DG: What doesn't?

JOHN: Well, ah, the land itself.

DG: But don't people own land?

JOHN: Part of it.

DG: What about the other parts?

You mean like going to the movies or something like that? Watching a movie, that's important. *Ed Rogers*

It's a great day! *Harry Katz*

I wish I had a cigarette. *Walter McGeorge*

Happy New Year! What day is today? (*DG: Friday*.) Oh. Joe Lewis—my uncle. *Larry Green*

Cookies, bananas and milk. *Ed Poindexter*

What do you have to do to get a cloud named after you?

Get drunk. *Charles Shay*

Speak to Jesus Christ. *Fergie*

Make a vacuum. *Andy Legrice*

I s'pose if you died, then they'd name it after you. *Frank Kanslasky*

You pray for sunshine. *Francis McElroy*

Wait until the rain comes. *John Fay*

I don't know, unless you jump with a parachute. *Jim Thibedeau*

There's a song, "Little White Cloud That Cried"—Johnny Ray used to sing it. *George Stingel*

Be in the sky. *Harry Katz*

Well, you probably have to get elevated to sainthood. There's a Saint Cloud, Minnesota, isn't there? *Bill Niemi*

You'd have to do something of national importance. *Ernie Brookings*

Get wacky, get mentally deranged. *Francis McElroy*

Damned if I know. *Larry Green*

Be an Indian. *Jack Mudurian*

JOHN: Belongs to someone else, I suppose.

Everything materially? (*DG: Yes.*) I would say so, yes.

—*Walter McGeorge*

I thought it did.

—*Jim Thibedeau*

How do I know, I don't live their life, I have all I can do to live my own life, don't you?

—*Walter Kieran*

It does, everything belongs to someone, sure.

—*John Fallon*

Well, these clothes belong to me. I got a suitcase belongin' to me. I've got a lot of clothes up in the attic belongin' to me.

—*John Fay*

Yes, everyone has their own personal property and their belongings. And they have their financial belongings. And they have their health. And they have their living. And also they have entertainment. They get plenty of food. And also plenty of musical entertainment. And that's about it.

—*Francis McElroy*

Yep. The man above. He put it here. He put the earth here and we've got to take care of it.

—*Andy Legrice*

Sure. You must have a possessions flag, in the navy they do. No one can take it away from you, that's stealin'.

—*George Stingel*

If you pay for it and buy it, it belongs to you. The clothes you're wearin' you bought and they belong to you. If you steal it, it still belongs to you! (*Laughs*)

—*Frank Wisnewski*

ED POINDEXTER: Yeah. I'm in bed right now, right?

DG: Yes.

ED: Yeah. Can we go to the luncheon today?

DG: No, we already ate.

ED: I ate already too. What time is it, nine o'clock?

DG: It's two.

ED: Yep.

ABE BERKOVER: No.

DG: What doesn't?

ABE: I don't know.

DG: Is it a legal matter?

ABE: No.

DG: What is it?

ABE: Government.

Ordinarily, yes. . . . Yes, theoretically.

—*Ernie Brookings*

I don't know nothin' about these questions you ask, they don't seem right. You ain't got the answers, so how'm I gonna tell you the right answer? If you knew the answers that'd be different. Geez, these quizzes are—(*shakes his head*)—I don't know! (*Laughs*) You ought to start on television, call it "Where Were You When I Wasn't Thcrc?"—give it a nice, fancy name. How come you don't make a television program, huh? You be the producer—you can be the star too. You know, you can even

Would you stop making sense if someone said you could?

VILJO LEHTO: Well, ah, yeah, I could stop making sense. I chased a bull out of the barn—that means I don't go kidding the people. If you go kidding people you're fooling yourself.

WALLY BAKER: That's the sixty-four-dollar question. Ask this guy here. (*Points at John Hodorowski*)

JOHN HODOROWSKI: That doesn't mean I'm gonna answer. That doesn't mean I don't have an answer—maybe I do and don't want to give it. Maybe if I give it, it'll scare him. (*Points at Wally*)

WALLY: (*Laughs*)

JOHN: I don't want to give it 'cause it'll scare me!

DG: Would you stop making sense if someone said you could?

ED ROGERS: If somebody said you couldn't make sense?

DG: Yeah.

ED: If somebody said you couldn't make sense.

DG: Yeah, that you could stop making sense.

ED: What do you mean, what do you mean? Real money, you mean, or what do you mean? Are you talking about money or what?

DG: No, sense—S-E-N-S-E.

ED: Oh, you mean the word, you mean, you mean the word sense!

DG: Yeah.

ED: Oh, sense.

DG: Yeah, if somebody said you could stop making sense, would you?

ED: (*Pause*) . . . Would I, would I, if somebody said, ah, you couldn't make sense?

DG: Yeah.

ED: No. I would say no.

write it. Get a new name, don't use Greenberger. Maybe David Green—a nice name, like Milton Berle. All you need is a backer. Get Stop & Shop, Zayre's, K-Mart, Bradlees—all them fellas got plenty of money, get them together. Sponsors.

—*Frank Kanslasky*

It should. We all started from nothing. "We all"—that's many of us. Many of us had a few nickels and dimes, but many of us didn't have anything, not a single cent. Not one red cent. Well, it *was* a red cent, I mean as red as the red shirt you've got on. It is a shirt, isn't it? (*DG: Yes.*) It has all the looks of a nice red shirt. I bet it cost eight or ten bucks, or it was given to you. Well, that's fair, F-A-I-R. I'm not a magician. In other words, I can't tell you everything. I'm not a dumbbell, but neither are any of you. We were put here for a reason. What that reason is, I don't know. We're all smart, or we think we're smart. We do what our forefathers taught us, which we had many. Some of them were brilliant men and some of them weren't. Some of them were brought up just like we were. Which is, you might say, a cigarette in one hand and nothin' in the other.

—*Fergie*

Well, if they, ah, own possession of it it must belong to them. The same as if I went into a place to buy somethin' and the man said, "That check is no good." And I said, "Well, I just put money in the bank, so it must be good." And he said, "Well I'll hold it and send it in when the bank opens."

—*Bernie Reagan*

Well, I imagine so. But probably in the final analysis we all belong to God.

—*Bill Niemi*

Yes, but the U.S. Government has it! (*Laughs*)

—*Abe Surgecoff*

BILL SEARS: No.

DG: What doesn't?

BILL: Cigarettes, that's all I can think of.

DG: Who do cigarettes belong to?

BILL: They belong to the office. Clothes.

DG: Who do they belong to?

BILL: They belong to the patients. That's all.

Yes, everything belongs to someone. Television, radio, Motorola radio in the dashboard of a car, boat, an airplane, motorcycle, motorskooter, motorbike, ice skates, skis, heater in the car, magic carpet—that's all, what else? Divan, bed, warm blanket, clock, food, smokin' pipes and I can't think of anything else. Automobile, bicycle, shirt, belt—hey, Dave, can you get me a new belt, I'm trying to get a new belt, I need a new belt—cigarette lighter, water fountain, bubbler, chewing gum, chewing tobacco, pipe tobacco, eyeglasses, hat, cap, ring on your fingers, wristwatch, cigarette, holder, cigarette pack in your shirt pocket, mustache, shoes, sneakers, bedroom slippers, brown corduroy bedroom slippers, ring—I already said ring—fountain pen, ballpoint pen, a barber's shears to cut men's hair, a washing machine that automatically washes your laundry for you, like in the laundromat. I'm going to get a drink of water.

—*Jack Mudurian*

How do you get a halo?

The sun. You get a halo. *Harry Katz*

You gotta be a saint, I think. You'd have to work your way up same as them, it's not easy, there's a lot of suffering. *Leo Germino*

Be honored. That's the thing they put over your hair, huh? Be honored and they put it over ya. Do a good deed. *Andy Legrice*

ERNIE BROOKINGS: Around the head, a halo?

DG: Yes.

ERNIE: I wouldn't know. Would a charming person be liable to produce a halo?

DG: I don't know.

ERNIE: I don't know either.

Don't get a haircut. *John Fay*

Make one, put it on your head! (*Laughs*) *Charles Fay*

Become an angel. *Frank Wisnewski*

When you're good. *John Fallon*

If you're a person and you're doin' like Christian or some kind of work that does good for other people, then usually after the person that it's about passes away, they take it before the church or the government boards to evaluate the person to some special sainthood value, usually in the church, isn't it? *Bill Niemi*

dp

I may not be the best Christian but I'm one of the kindest men in America. If I won a million dollars in the lottery I'd give it all away to the homeless and hungry. All I'm looking for right now is friends from eighteen to sixty, both men and women, because I'm very lonely. If anyone wants to get in touch with me get the number from the Schenectady phone book, I'm down at the YMCA. I've got a very good reputation. *Henry Turner*

dp

If you were stranded on an island, what three things would you want to have with you?

I'd want my husband, Elvis Presley and the Salvation Army.

—Daphne Matthews

My wife and children.

—Larry Green

A woman, food and smokin' equipment.

—Walter McGeorge

You'd have water to drink and somethin' to eat. (*DG: And one more thing.*) And you could have a girl, maybe not always.

—George Stingel

Swimmin', put a lifeguard on, and, ah, put a bathin' suit on.

—Abe Surgecoff

I'd like to have happiness, contentment and be left alone in solitary confinement, and to be enjoyed by everybody. And I'd like to have enough to eat and enough musical contentment.

—Francis McElroy

A mermaid, eats—food and drink

—Andy Legrice

Probably some kind of a tent and some kind of food supplies and some kind of walkie-talkie or communications equipment so you could get in touch with somebody. That would be a terrible thing to happen in this day and age, to be stranded on an island.

—Bill Niemi

A woman, something to drink and cigars.

—*John Fallon*

Food, water, doctor.

—*Abe Berkover*

A flashlight, a gun and food.

—*Charles Shea*

Food and a Bible and a map of that area.

—*Ernie Brookings*

How do you find your way home?

Well, I don't know, my husband said something about the sun, about which direction it's coming from. It was something about the sun but I don't remember exactly what it was.

—*Daphne Matthews*

I follow the cow path, the cows know the way to the barn. And some of the cows have a bell on 'em. I'm speakin' of farmin' now. (*DG: How do you find your way home not on a farm?*) It depends on what kind of a night it is, if it's a nice moonlight night I can find my way home good, but if it's dark I just lie down under a tree and go to sleep.

—*Viljo Lehto*

Sometimes not so good! (*Laughs*) When it's slippery! I remember some days I couldn't find my way home when I had a couple, a-couple-a-couple-a—you know what I mean!

—*John Hodorowski*

EDDIE RUTTER: I had a minister investigated for Communism. I was the instigator of it. And oh, that minister got really boiling mad over that! He was really a good minister, though, beyond that.

DG: Did he get in trouble?

EDDIE: Well, not right away. I didn't push it no further. You see, when I was discharged from the army, that was in 1943, and they told me that anytime anybody bothered me any or didn't give me proper satisfaction to let them know and they would take ahold of the situation and they would straighten it out.

DG: And did they?

EDDIE: They straightened out quite a few deals.

DG: What made you suspicious of this minister in the first place?

EDDIE: Well, it was just an idea that came into my mind.

I don't know where I'm gonna be livin' in the future, but I do know that livin' in a motel right now is my reward for telling God I love him so much I would die for him. I mean it, that's my reward—put that down, Henry Turner. *Henry Turner*

What's déjà vu?

Deja boo. It could be disastrous. Boo, B-O-O. It could be disastrous, depending on the nature of the boo. *Ernie Brookings*

French food. *Larry Green*

A good drunken party—a celebration, right? *Andy Legrice*

I don't know, it might be whiskey. *David Brewer*

I don't know. Ten dollars? In American money is that ten dollars? *Abe Surgecoff*

Perfume? *Bill LaGasse*

It's quite an involved process, really. But I'd say familiarity would be the basic thing.

—Bill Hughes

Probably you have to have your body in good shape. You have to have good eyesight so you can see your way home.

—Bill Niemi

Ask the police department, they'll help you. They might even give you a ride home.

—Leo Germino

Pay money in the elevator.

—Abe Surgecoff

That would depend upon location and distance. Follow the signs and use a road map.

—Ernie Brookings

If you get lost, you stay there and wait and they take you home. You sit pretty. If you're lost, you just sit there.

—Larry Green

Well, I just happen to know the way and I just go the way I know, that's back to my room.

—Eddie Rutter

How do you find your way home?! You can always find that, unless you're drunk or somethin'.

—Roy Elliott

I just follow my nose. (*Takes out handkerchief and blows his nose.*)

—Wallace Baker

dp

What's the most valuable thing you ever lost?

MARY PIESZCZOCH: A beaded purse.

DG: I'll try and find it.

MARY: David, you'll never find it. I had my sister on a sled and she was holding it and dropped in the snow. We used to make beautiful beaded purses.

DG: You made it?

MARY: Sure I made it. Ask me what I haven't made! That was every bit of sixty years ago.

Well, to me it was valuable—it was a letter written to us extolling the virtues of my son from the superintendent of schools. He said it could be used as a letter of recommendation anytime in his life. It told that he was not only good scholastically, but he had good character as well. I lost it somewhere. It fell out of my pocket, to me it was valuable.

—Herman Seftel

My daughter, in '48.

—Dora Gurkewitz

Materially, I lost a pair of candlesticks. They were taken out of my house and I valued them dearly because they were a gift from my mother for my anniversary.

—Ann Stark

I lost a diamond ring, right in my own house.

—Sadye Weinstein

Well, it's a French word, but it means like a sixth sense, like you can go beyond. In other words, that you can predict and tell things. They say everyone has a little déjà vu, but some can do quite a lot with it.
Jeanne Malone

That's a foreign word and I can't say as I know what it is. Wouldn't that word be a French word? (*DG: Yes.*) I kinda had an idea it was, but I don't know what it is. *Eddie Rutter*

I don't know. *Roy Elliott*

You're never gonna find out what that means 'cause that's mispronounced. That's a mix-up, mixed up word, two of 'em. *John Hodorowski*

No kabeesh. *Wallace Baker*

That's French and I ain't gonna read it 'cause if I do I'm as bad as they are.
Viljo Lehto

That's not said right, now wait a minute, that's Polish. (*DG: What's it mean?*) It's all mixed up and I can't answer that 'cause it would only be my opinion and it might not be right.
John Hodorowski

I've experienced it, mostly when I was younger. That's something that maybe you lose your sensitivity to when you get older. *Bill Hughes*

dp

There's God, the son and the Holy Ghost—it's a three-in-one God! *Henry Turner*

dp

There ain't no heaven. What you think they got up there—carrots? No! You think they got Cadillac cars up there? This is heaven right here. Look up at the ceiling—the building, the grass, this is heaven. You're livin' in heaven. You die and you go up to hell, up to the sun and you burn up in hell. *Frank Kanslasky*

dp

Well, I would say my husband.

—Molly Segal

FRED DELAP: I haven't lost too much. . . . Oh! My mother!

EDDIE RUTTER: Well, naturally it's when you lose your father and mother and so on.

FRED: Yeah, it's the worst thing, father and mother.

DAPHNE MATTHEWS: A lot of pictures. Well, everything—I had a fire and I lost everything. A thousand dollars' worth of furniture—everything went up in smoke.

DG: When was this?

DAPHNE: Nineteen seventy-three, December 19th, the day before my husband's birthday. Nice birthday present, huh? We were out on the street.

My mother.

—George Vrooman

When I lost my mind in 1953, and the most valuable thing I possess now is my mind. My mind is getting better. I almost lost my mind in 1953 and I almost completely lost my mind in 1969 and 1983. In 1983 a five-year-old kid had more intelligence than me.

—Henry Turner

I ain't had nothing valuable!

—Viljo Lehto

My smell, odor! Put anything down, I don't give a damn what you put down!

—John Hodorowski

My father and mother and three brothers. I'm the only one left.

—Wally Baker

My television set, it was stolen. I spent close to four hundred dollars for it.

—Barbara Katz

I suppose, thinking of it very abstractly now, my early conceits and my early, ah—what's the word I need?—your early illusions and early naivete.

—Bill Hughes

How do you get good luck?

By not making enemies.

—Jack Mudurian

Just by listenin' to whom you hear.

—Leo Germino

Well, it just comes naturally, I suppose. Sometimes it comes to you. Some people have good luck and some have bad—er—different.

—Ed Rogers

If someone's good to you.

—Abe Surgecoff

Good livin'. See if you can dig up a cigarette from somebody, will ya? I like to smoke after I eat, I enjoy it.

—Walter Kieran

I'm not junk, God made me.
Henry Turner

DG: Arthur, how're you doing?

ARTHUR: It's very puzzling.

DG: What's puzzling?

ARTHUR: This existence. The way we live.

DG: You're sounding pretty philosophical.

ARTHUR: What do you mean, phisolog—philogos—philo—?

dp

At this point, I'm just gonna cool it. One coal can't burn very long by itself. *Henry Turner*

You know, years ago in the Catholic church you used to go into a booth and confess to the priest. But you can bow your head any goddamn place and get cleaned up. *Wally Baker*

As long as there's Bible laws they can throw them anyplace. *Eddie Rutter*

There's only one God, but there's lots of devils. There might be millions. *Frank Kanslasky*

Herbie Caldwell: Christ, I'm caught here like a mouse in a trap.

DG: How do you figure?

HERBIE: No, no. I was only kidding.

Lead a clean life, I guess, what the hell can I tell ya? Lead a clean life and mind your own business, and with any luck you'll have good luck.

—Frank Wisnewski

I don't know—if you're lucky you're lucky.

—Eugene Hickey

By prayin' to the Lord.

—John Fallon

Playin' fair and honest.

—Andy Legrice

I don't know, I guess that nobody can do that. You ain't got to write that down!

—Gene Edwards

I was born on a lucky day, Friday the thirteenth. (*DG: I thought that was an unlucky day.*) Well, I was born on Friday the thirteenth, so there must be something good in there.

—Bill Niemi

That's your fate.

—Gil Greene

Just comes to you. (*DG: What causes it to come to you?*) I don't know, nature.

—Charles Shea

Pray for it. (*DG: What kind of prayer?*) Lord's Prayer.

—Harry Katz

By livin' right.

—Harold Farrington

It all depends on the previous involvements. You get good luck from previous actions and previous factors.

—Ernie Brookings

Through faith—F-A-I-T-H. And also a love of music.

—Francis McElroy

WALTER MCGEORGE: Yeah, how do you get it?

DG: How do you?

WALTER: I don't know.

DG: Any ideas?

WALTER: Not the slightest. Pray, I guess.

Knit. I'm making afghans now. I was makin' hats, now I'm makin' afghans.

—Herbert Wilson

I pitch horseshoes.

—Jerry Celeste

Oh, I don't know, whatever comes to mind, I guess.

—Alice Bitowski

I do housework.

—Margie Hurwich

Live cautiously, think before you make a move.

—Carmen Smemo

Do harm to nobody and nobody does harm to you, it's as simple as that. Exactly what you give is what you get in life—that's good luck, not gambling.

—Fred Delap

I've got a good story for you:

In 1969, this was in September, I was in Northside, the old hospital in Utica, New York, and I came home on a visit. I was so sick I couldn't do nothin', except dress myself and feed myself. And I went to the bathroom and I don't know what happened to me, but I remember vomiting blood. I told my mother about it, they rushed me to St. Clair's Hospital. They examined me by X-ray and they found I had holes in my esophagus. Five doctors said I was going to die a horrible death. A man prayed to Jesus and Jesus healed my holes and I lived. In other words, I'm a walking miracle, I should've died in 1969 but I lived. I'm the only person who ever lived with holes in their esophagus—everyone else who ever had it before died a horrible death. *Henry Turner*

The big truck's gone and so am I. *Herbie Caldwell*

dp

Perseverance—you shouldn't give up the ship. Like they say, don't give up the ship till you see the whites of their eyes. *John Hodorowski*

dp

DG: John, What's up?

JOHN FAY: New York! New Jersey! North Carolina!

dp

You can't be perfect holding things in your hand all the time, you've got to drop something once in a while. *Gene Edwards*

dp

Just live, that's all, and hope for the best the next day. One day at a time, just live it out.

—*John Hodorowski*

Live by the Golden Rule, I'd say that.

—*Herb Farrell*

Well, I can tell you how not to get it—be kind and nice to people. I can tell you that because I've tried it. The people have changed, it's not like how it used to be.

—*Bill Hughes*

I don't have no good luck. I haven't had any good luck since April.

—*Viljo Lehto*

Well, whatever you estimate is right and so on. I use the Bible as much as I possibly can.

—*Eddie Rutter*

Keep your fingers crossed! (*Laughs*)

—*Fred Delap*

Jesus! I no do nothing!

—*Sam Vara*

A four leaf clover. Rabbit's foot, which I don't believe in. (*DG: What do you believe in?*) God, naturally.

—*Homer LaViolette*

Buy yourself a horseshoe.

—*Wallace Baker*

JEANNE MALONE: You don't get it, you either have it or you don't. It'll find you.

DAPHNE MATTHEWS: I guess you have to pray.

JEANNE: A lot of people say you shouldn't walk under ladders or have black cats.

DAPHNE: I was raised with black cats, I love 'em.

JEANNE: Look at you, Daphne, you have bad luck.

DAPHNE: If it wasn't for bad luck I wouldn't have no luck at all.

GEORGE VROOMAN: Just try to live right.

DAPHNE: You get into the ring and sock it to 'em!

BARBARA KATZ: How I get good luck is believe in myself. I believe I can do something and I go do it.

JEANNE: You can't get it, you can't catch it.

BARBARA: You can't—you have to believe in yourself.

JEANNE: Luck is just a state that people believe in. Being grateful and luck have a lot to do with each other, I think.

How do you get good luck? By waitin'! By waitin' and bein' an escape artist.

—*Jack Mudurian*

My shoveling days are over, Davy baby.

—*Frank Wisnewski*

Keep up with the faith.
Charlie Johanson

You got me caught here like a pair of pants. *Herbie Caldwell*

Ask not what, but what for.
Ed Poindexter

dp

I always say "so long," I never say "goodbye." Why?—I'll see you again.

—*Ken Eglin*

William “Fergie” Ferguson

dp

About the Author

David B. Greenberger grew up in Erie, Pennsylvania. He studied painting at the Massachusetts College of Art. In 1979, he began conducting the interviews which make up *The Duplex Planet* magazine. *The Duplex Planet* continues to grow in popularity and circulation and has also been adapted into comic books, recordings and dramatic performances. David Greenberger currently resides in upstate New York with his daughter Norabelle.

For more information, please send a self-addressed stamped envelope to *The Duplex Planet,* P.O. Box 1230, Saratoga Springs, NY 12866.